D0387157

The Dollarization Discipline

HOW SMART COMPANIES CREATE CUSTOMER VALUE ... AND PROFIT FROM IT

Jeffrey J. Fox
Richard C. Gregory

WILEY

John Wiley & Sons, Inc.

Copyright © 2004 by Jeffrey J. Fox and Richard C. Gregory. All rights reserved.

Published by John Wiley & Sons, Inc., Hoboken, New Jersey.
Published simultaneously in Canada.

No part of this publication may be reproduced, stored in a retrieval system, or transmitted in any form or by any means, electronic, mechanical, photocopying, recording, scanning, or otherwise, except as permitted under Section 107 or 108 of the 1976 United States Copyright Act, without either the prior written permission of the Publisher, or authorization through payment of the appropriate per-copy fee to the Copyright Clearance Center, Inc., 222 Rosewood Drive, Danvers, MA 01923, (978) 750-8400, fax (978) 646-8600, or on the web at www.copyright.com. Requests to the Publisher for permission should be addressed to the Permissions Department, John Wiley & Sons, Inc., 111 River Street, Hoboken, NJ 07030, (201) 748-6011, fax (201) 748-6008.

Limit of Liability/Disclaimer of Warranty: While the publisher and author have used their best efforts in preparing this book, they make no representations or warranties with respect to the accuracy or completeness of the contents of this book and specifically disclaim any implied warranties of merchantability or fitness for a particular purpose. No warranty may be created or extended by sales representatives or written sales materials. The advice and strategies contained herein may not be suitable for your situation. The publisher is not engaged in rendering professional services, and you should consult a professional where appropriate. Neither the publisher nor author shall be liable for any loss of profit or any other commercial damages, including but not limited to special, incidental, consequential, or other damages.

For general information on our other products and services please contact our Customer Care Department within the United States at (800) 762-2974, outside the United States at (317) 572-3993 or fax (317) 572-4002.

Designations used by companies to distinguish their products are often claimed by trademarks. In all instances where the author or publisher is aware of a claim, the product names appear in Initial Capital letters. Readers, however, should contact the appropriate companies for more complete information regarding trademarks and registration.

Wiley also publishes its books in a variety of electronic formats. Some content that appears in print may not be available in electronic books. For more information about Wiley products, visit our web site at www.Wiley.com.

Library of Congress Cataloging-in-Publication Data:
Fox, Jeffrey J., 1945–
    The dollarization discipline : how smart companies create customer value . . . and profit from it / Jeffrey J. Fox, Richard C. Gregory.
        p. cm.
    ISBN 0-471-65950-9 (cloth)
    1. Marketing—Management.   2. Sales management.   3. Value added.
    4. Consumer satisfaction—Evaluation.   I. Gregory, Richard C., 1965–
    II. Title.
    HF5415.15.F69   2004
    658.8—dc22
2004007665

Printed in the United States of America.

10 9 8 7 6 5 4 3 2 1

*Rick Gregory dedicates this book
to the team at MKM Group, especially the CEO.*

Jeffrey Fox dedicates this book to Marlene.

*The authors would like to acknowledge
Doris Michaels and Ben Salmon at the DSM Agency,
and Matthew Holt and the rest of the team
at John Wiley & Sons, Inc.*

Contents

Preface

This book is about a concept that, on its surface, is simple to comprehend. It is about understanding the *financial* impacts a product or service has on its buyer. Readers may conclude this means the book is about "total cost of ownership." In fact, it is . . . in part. But it is also about something bigger. Traditionally, as the phrase suggests, "total cost of ownership" focuses only on *cost*. Cost reduction and cost avoidance are important aspects of dollarization, but they are often only half the story. Dollarization also requires measuring the financial impact of noncost benefits. Benefits such as increased market share, increased sales volume, and increased pricing power also must be dollarized.

Further, companies often use "total cost of ownership" and similar concepts in limited circumstances. An important goal of this book is to demonstrate how dollarization should be a *discipline* that organizations apply across a broad set of sales, marketing, and management activities. Most marketers would agree that a business should be customer-focused or customer-driven. Dollarization forces companies to behave this way. It does so by helping companies maintain steadfast focus on the *financial* performance that is the ultimate arbiter of their customers' success.

So while dollarization may be an easily understood concept, it can be difficult to put into practice. But our experience in helping great companies make dollarization work has convinced us that it is well worth the effort.

Introductory Notes

A NOTE ON TERMINOLOGY

Throughout this book, we use terminology such as "supplier," "vendor," "customer," and "product" to describe the buyer/seller business relationship. These words may suggest a focus on tangible products, exclusive of intangible or intellectual services. This is not the case. Nearly every point we make in this book can be applied to either a product *or* a service, without distinction. We find that tangible product examples allow us to more clearly articulate the observations we seek to share, and we use them solely for this purpose. Several chapters and specific service examples should clarify this.

A NOTE ON CASE HISTORIES

Every case example we use in this book is based on an actual business situation. In many cases, the companies involved have chosen to remain anonymous, preferring to keep their competitive strategies nonattributed. For these cases, we have substituted fictitious company names. The use of such invented names is indicated at the start of each of these cases.

We thank all the many excellent companies, managers, marketers, and salespeople who have made these events happen and have shared them with us.

INTRODUCTION TO DOLLARIZATION

There is hardly anything in the world that some man cannot make a little worse and sell a little cheaper, and the people who consider price only are this man's lawful prey.

—John Ruskin

It's unwise to pay too much, but it is more unwise to pay too little. When you pay too much you lose a little money—that is all; When you pay too little, you sometimes lose everything, because the thing you bought was incapable of doing the thing it was bought to do.

—John Ruskin

Chapter 1

Getting Started with Dollarization

The weekend arrives and you're shopping for paint to freshen up the outside of your home. You arrive at the local paint store to find many choices. You narrow the possibilities down to two: Product X costs $12 a gallon; product Y costs $20 a gallon. Which paint should you buy?

The salesperson greets you with a warm smile. She watches you deliberate, then says, "I strongly recommend product Y. Its price may be higher, but it will last eight years, while the other paint will last four at best. That means that over eight years, you'd have to buy product X twice, for a total of $24 a gallon, versus just $20 a gallon for product Y. In reality, product Y costs less!"

You reply, "That's very interesting, but I'm preparing to sell my home, so I don't care about how long this paint will last. I think I'll go with product X for $12."

The salesperson listens and responds, "I understand, but I think product Y is still your best choice. You see, product Y contains 50 percent more pigment, which results in better coverage than product X. This means you will need to apply only one coat to your house. Product X will require at least two coats. This will also cut your labor costs in half. Plus, you are guaranteed that your house will look freshly painted, which will improve your success in selling your home. Wouldn't you agree that an extra $8 per gallon is a great investment to sell your house at the price you want?"

Finally, you decide. The $20 paint is actually less expensive than the $12 paint.

The logic in this example seems obvious, yet every day, sellers and marketers lose sales because they unintentionally allow customers to believe that their higher-priced products truly cost more than their competitors'. And every day, customers choose low-priced products despite the higher total cost that will actually result.

Consider another familiar scenario: When buying a car, there are many costs and considerations to weigh. There is, of course, the *price*, which typically gets 99 percent of the buyer's attention. But there are also fuel costs, maintenance costs, finance costs, insurance costs, personal property taxes, resale value, and on and on. In reality, price is but one of many costs to consider when weighing the decision to buy a car.

When businesses make purchases, too often they are myopic and overemphasize the importance of price. They overlook (sometimes inadvertently, sometimes intentionally) the many other financial consequences of choosing one offering over another. This is a failure on the buyer's part, because it may very well result in financial harm to the organization. But more importantly, it is a failure on the seller's part because the seller has missed the chance to demonstrate the true financial impact that could be provided to the customer.

As with house paint and cars, the meaningful way to compare the cost of two offerings is by evaluating the *total cost* of using each. In order to help customers to understand the true net cost of your product, you must *dollarize the product's true value*.

WHAT IS DOLLARIZATION?

This book is about a concept we coined called *dollarization*. Dollarization can be defined many ways depending on its usage, but the essential concept is:

Dollarization   The translation of the benefits a product or service delivers to a customer into the dollars-and-cents financial impact to that customer.

In other words, dollarization is a method for converting the ubiquitous buzzword "value-added" into real money. It is *figuring out what your offering is really worth — in dollars and cents — to your customer.*

Dollarization is a management discipline that is missing in many sales and marketing organizations. Its impact can be great, and its applications are many.

Dollarization is not an entirely new concept. For years, good companies have understood the need to express their value in financial terms. But even the best firms tend to utilize a dollarized approach to sales and marketing only in selected situations. Or they apply it too narrowly. For example, some companies use the concept called "lowest cost of ownership." This is a good concept — if the seller really does the math — but it is often half the dollarized story. The other half of the dollarization story is calculating the top-line revenues (and consequent margin dollars) that *a seller's product can generate* for the buyer. If the seller's product enables the customer's company to get its product to market faster, or to outperform the customer's competition, or to raise prices, then the customer's return on the seller's product can be enormous.

Sellers of big-ticket items are often forced (by customer capital appropriation policies) to demonstrate the return on investment (ROI) for their wares. Other industries dollarize because the need is self-evident: For example, jet engine makers compete on fuel efficiency because small changes in miles per gallon can have enormous impact on the operating costs of their airline customers. But more often than not, dollarization is not even considered by the seller.

Nor is dollarization demanded by enough customers. The foremost mission of a business is to create value for its owners. Managers of a business have a fiduciary responsibility to the owners to manage in a fashion that can be reasonably expected to create value. And when shareholders discuss "value," they are talking about the *financial* value of the share price, the cash flow, the dividend paid.

When a business operates, its managers must align the available resources to create value. It follows, then, that every expenditure made by a company should be made with an eye toward value creation.

When a company needs to make a major infrastructure investment—a new piece of capital equipment or a new software platform, for example—it is common for managers to conduct some level of due diligence and economic analysis to assure themselves that their investment will provide the best return. But somewhere down the purchasing chain, after the capital goods but long before the paper clips and toilet paper, many managers abandon this financial discipline. They see those remaining products as inconsequential and focus not on value but on price. Worse yet, the *marketers and sellers* of these products succumb to this negative belief and complain that their so-called commodity products are judged only on price. But even seemingly inconsequential products can be dollarized. Whether through subtle product design or performance differences, or through packaging, delivery, or service elements, any product a business buys *can* be dollarized.

With this book, we will explain how dollarization can help your company better understand, articulate, and profit from the value you create for your customers and clients. Dollarization should become a standing discipline that guides your thinking

Note: Our discussion of dollarization is intended to help companies understand and demonstrate the true value delivered by their offerings. This knowledge can be used for direct advantage in the marketplace, and can be used for a variety of strategic purposes. Occasionally, we are approached by firms that hope dollarization can in some way help obfuscate the true market situation, and thereby provide an opportunity for an offering to shine brighter to potential customers than reality might warrant. While there are certainly many legitimate sales and marketing uses of dollarization that we believe can improve a seller's chances of success, we do not intend it to serve as an illegitimate smoke screen.

If you tell lies about a product, you will be found out by the Government, which will prosecute you, or by the consumer, who will punish you by not buying your product a second time.[1]

—David Ogilvy

about pricing, selling, positioning, new product development, and nearly every other area of your sales and marketing.

Companies that truly create economic value for their customers *deserve to share in that value*. The price premium a value-creating firm can command enables the company to invest in continued innovation and to commit resources to generate even further value. Dollarization enables companies to afford the necessary investments required to perpetuate the creation of customer value.

Too many companies create value but don't keep their rightful share. We hope after reading this book you will do otherwise . . . and dollarize.

Chapter 2

Value Is a Number

Just as languages have leaped across borders and diseases have jumped from one species to another, somewhere in the history of business, the word *value* escaped the finance department and migrated into the lexicon of sales and marketing.

But finance people live in a world of numbers. Accordingly, their notion of value is true. They talk of book value, discounted value, asset value. When finance and accounting people talk value, they talk about financial value. They talk about dollars, cents, euros, yuan, and yen. If value can't be calculated on an accountant's HP-12C calculator, it does not exist. But when the term *value* leaves the realm of finance and accounting and heads to sales and marketing, a loosening of definitions occurs.

In sales and marketing, *value* takes the form of value-added (or more succinctly, value-add), value chain, value proposition, or value engineering. In concept alone, these are all legitimate business ideas. However, in execution, they seldom meet the breathless promise to which they aspire. When sales and marketing people talk value, they use words and rarely use numbers. The words they use lack precision.

When explaining this concept to managers, we often use the

analogy of a recruiting dialogue between a football coach and his scout.

> *Scout:* Coach, you really ought to draft this kid. He's fast.
> *Coach:* How fast?
> *Scout:* Really fast! And also, he's huge.
> *Coach:* How huge?
> *Scout:* Really, really huge. He's as big as a mountain! And guess what—he's really strong, too.

And on it goes.

If instead the scout had come from the finance side of the organization, he might report as follows:

> *Scout:* This prospect runs the 40 in 4.3 seconds, he's 6 foot 3 and weighs 240, and he bench-presses 400 pounds.

Subjectivity and uncertainty are now eliminated from the coach's assessment. The recruit is a tenth of a second faster and 10 pounds heavier than the next kid. He's the one.

But in business, fine companies fall short in defining their value. In just the past few months, we've observed the following vague statements of value by top firms:

> "Valeo adds technology. Valeo adds value."
> "Value our Value-Added Valves."
> "The Value-Added Specialist."
> "When Value Matters."

In fact, a recent Google search for the phrase "How We Add Value" produced more than 1,500 hits! (The phrase "add value" by itself generated 1.3 million hits!) It would seem that some enterprising web design guru has persuaded an army of website designers that all sites must have a "How We Add Value" section.

We don't point out these uses of *value* in sales and marketing to ridicule. In fact, the mere presence of one of the many value

---

What Exactly Is Value?

The word *value* gets lots of play in business, but what does it mean, and how does it apply to businesses? Several definitions are listed in the dictionary. One set of definitions addresses personal, moral, and ethical value. These refer to value as a "principle, standard, or quality considered worthwhile or desirable." This aspect of value is important in the overall governance and conduct of companies, but it is not the definition of value that truly drives businesses.

Another set of definitions describes value as economic value. In this realm, value is defined as:

- The worth of a thing.
- An assigned or computed numerical value.
- Monetary or material worth.

This definition is more in line with legendary value investor Benjamin Graham's approach to value, where through careful analysis, investors seek to identify companies with intrinsic economic value that is greater than the current share price.

The value described by the first set of definitions is required to keep the world of business civilized. Shareholder activism and a huge and growing body of legislation and regulation are in place to sustain these values. The value described by the economic definitions is required to keep companies *profitable*.

phrases at least indicates that someone at each of these firms understands—at some level—that they are in fact in business to
create value for their customers. Instead, our intention is to help
companies convert that understanding into a meaningful way of
executing business strategy.

Unfortunately, the word *value* has become yet another

Value As in Cheap

While the term *value* may be used too casually in describing
the economic impact companies generate for their customers,
another egregious area of misuse can be seen in the growing
category of low-priced products now known as the "value"
category. As Ralf Leszinski and Michael Marn of McKinsey &
Company accurately observe: " 'Value pricing' is too often
misused as a synonym for low price or bundled price."[1]

Certain carmakers, retailers, and other purveyors of low-
priced products scream "value" in an attempt to avoid the
derogative "cheap." In some cases, so-called value-priced
products do in fact create value. This is because value can cut
both ways. The delivery of significant dollarized value in ex-
change for a premium price may leave the customer with excess "net value." Meanwhile, a so-called value-priced product
may deliver much less dollarized value, but if the price is low
enough, it may in fact create the same net value for the customer (total dollarized value minus price).

However, more often than not, the value-priced product is
a low-price/low-value offering meant to appeal to human fru-
gality and limited purchasing power. Customers must guard
against *cheap* products masquerading in "value" clothing.

Accurate comparisons of "cheap" and "value" cannot be
made without first understanding the dollarized value of
each offering.

meaningless sound in the cluttered language of [...] "quality," "reengineering," "paradigm shift," and [...] buzzwords before it, the word *value* receives muc[...] energy, but little sound execution. Business plans, marketing plans, and sales plans promote how companies will "leverage the value" they create for customers, but rarely do they state what that value is worth. It strikes us that some managers believe that if they *say* they create value enough times, it might actually become true or the customer will bite and buy.

The solution is an approach to sales and marketing that goes beyond articulating features and benefits, but in fact calculates the economic value a customer receives from a product or service, and therefore enables the seller to price the product or service as a true reflection of that value. This approach is called dollarization.

BUSINESSES DON'T BUY, THEY INVEST

Let's back up a bit. We're talking about turning value into a number. But first, let's take a conceptual look at why this works in the business of sales and marketing. In their 1996 book *Power Pricing*, Robert Dolan and Hermann Simon concisely describe the dynamics of price and value:

> Price is the economic sacrifice a customer makes to acquire a product or a service. The customer always compares this sacrifice with his perception of the product's value. Price and value are the cornerstones of every economic transaction. In essence, a customer buys a product or service only if its perceived value—measured in money terms—is greater than the price. If selecting from several alternatives,

the customer prefers the one offering the highest net value, i.e., the greatest differential of perceived value over price.[2]

Dolan and Simon hit the nail on the head, but in our view, their description stops a few steps short. They do not address the challenge of *how* to quantify and articulate "perceived value—measured in money terms." (In fairness, the purpose of Dolan and Simon's discussion is to set up a presentation of their excellent microeconomic pricing analysis, not to explain how value is communicated.)

"Perceived value—measured in money terms" is what dollarization is all about. In other words, this book is about a very simple idea: Every time a company sells something, it must at some point present its price to the customer. In many cases, the customer also looks at alternative companies, all of which must also present prices for their offerings.

But there is a critical disconnect in most business-to-business sales and marketing. When it comes to discussing price, the facts are clear. The seller offers a price in dollars and cents, sometimes even fractions of cents, with great precision. There is no ambiguity about the price.

But when it comes to presenting what the customer gets in return for that price, the same seller hurls a list of features, benefits, and promises. (See Figure 2.1.) The seller claims superlatives such as best, fastest, strongest, most robust, most reliable, most effective, most experienced, most dependable, and so on. The marketer hopes the presentation of these claims sufficiently persuades the prospective customer to part with more money in return. In the end, the customer is left to make a financial decision: "What price is worth paying?" Customers are forced to make this financial decision by assessing *nonfinancial* arguments.

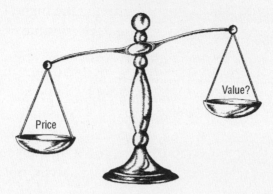

FIGURE 2.1 Without Dollarization, Comparison of Price and Value Is Impossible

Most marketers and salespeople stop short of translating their story into numbers. Instead of helping a customer understand that the $4 price will produce $7 in net savings, or that the $1 million investment will yield a total return of $4 million, they use words that are simply inadequate. To use a baseball analogy, this is akin to a sports page reporting that "the Red Sox scored four runs and the Yankees played really well" (without telling the reader if the Yankees scored two runs or eight)!

Today, most customers are left to apply a strange calculus of experience, analysis, and guesswork to determine the value side of the pricing equation: *What is the value of the benefits received, and therefore how much should be invested in the product or service?* Many companies have become skilled at doing this analysis themselves, but most, in our experience, have not. In the absence of such knowledge, many customers set minimum performance criteria and then refuse to pay extra for any so-called value-added. For example, a public school building committee could decide that a single criterion would qualify a brand of door hardware for consideration: the ability to meet minimum durability standards as defined by government rating agencies. All brands meeting this criterion would compete on the basis of lowest price only. In framing their decisions this way, the committee forgoes the opportunity to consider higher-priced hardware that might far exceed the minimum performance required. This exposes the school committee to saving on the purchase price while risking higher long-term costs of maintenance, security, and overall ownership.

Other, more conservative organizations may overinvest in the hope of scoring greater value, only to throw good money away. This is like the driver who assumes that buying 92 octane gasoline is worth the extra 30 cents a gallon without truly understanding the performance difference between regular and premium fuel.

If you take nothing else away from this book, we hope you take this: Businesses do not buy; they invest. Companies do not wake up in the morning and exclaim, "Let's go buy $10,000 worth of fasteners today" (or $15,000 worth of software, or 10 hours of their lawyers' time). On the contrary, companies don't want to spend one penny on any fasteners. But if they need fasteners, they must invest in fasteners. And the customer's need reflects a problem. The fastener solution can always be dollarized.

Every time a company makes a purchase decision, it is committing company capital. In theory, that capital is constantly being allocated and reallocated to achieve the best available return. But in our experience, too few companies exercise this discipline for all purchases. And far fewer companies market and sell in a way that permits customers to understand the economic value provided in return for the investment.

Whether you sell industrial products, legal services, high-tech components, or enterprise software solutions, you must understand why your customers should invest in you. Do you enable your customer to reduce warranty claim costs? Eliminate costly liability exposure? Gain new market share? Eliminate overhead costs? Whatever it is you do, you must map exactly how your offering translates to value for your customer's business.

DOLLARIZATION AND BUYING MOTIVATION

Before trying to dollarize your value, it is helpful to consider one other piece of fundamental buying theory. Why do people buy things, and when does dollarization make sense?

There are two fundamental reasons that drive all purchase decisions: People buy either to *feel good* or to *solve a problem*. Consumer purchases are often driven largely by feel-good reasons. For example, you might choose clothing based on how it makes you feel or look. You might select a bottle of wine because its taste is pleasing. You might give money to a charity because that will make you feel worthwhile. Or you might buy a stereo because of the rich sound it produces. You probably won't be interested in the financial return on your investment in these items though (well . . . maybe the wine has a dollarized value for some collectors). Consumer purchases are also driven by the need to solve problems, such as buying a minivan to transport children, or buying a dishwasher to eliminate washing dishes by hand. But because our personal lives are not strictly profit-driven enterprises, not every personal problem we solve can be dollarized. (There are, however, many cases when dollarization does work when selling to consumers. See Chapter 16 for more on this.)

Economists sometimes refer to these feel-good elements as "nonfinancial costs." This may be an accurate portrayal of the

TABLE 2.1   Two Sides to Solving Customer Problems

Examples of Avoidance of Loss	*Examples of Chance for Gain*
• Reduce cost of materials.	• Increase sales.
• Reduce downtime.	• Increase prices.
• Reduce labor costs.	• Expand market share.
• Reduce regulatory penalties.	• Enter new markets.
• Reduce product liability costs.	• Earn new customers.
• Eliminate manufacturing waste.	• Enable new products.

role they play as consumers consider trade-offs between various purchase options. However, we have never seen a company announce lower quarterly earnings due to unexpectedly high non-financial costs.

So while feel-good or nonfinancial costs may drive consumer purchase decisions, *the primary driver behind nearly all business expenditures is the need to solve some type of problem.* Further, in business, the solution to a problem represents either the avoidance of loss or the chance for gain (see Table 2.1). Both of these can be measured in dollars and cents . . . or dollarized.

Chapter 3

Why Dollarize?

It would be hypocritical if we did not make some attempt to dollarize the value of the ideas in this book. Why should an organization make the effort required to put these concepts into action?

It is instructive to first consider value in a broader context. Again, Robert Dolan and Hermann Simon provide an excellent framework:

> "Value" refers to that created for the various stakeholders, including the stockholders. The marketing strategy is the mediating process for creating this corporate "value." A corporation has value for its stockholders only if it is able to take a set of inputs and create value for its chosen customers. The *value creation* part of the firm's marketing strategy is the design, distribution of, and communication about its products and services to its chosen customers. Pricing strategy is the *value extraction* piece of the marketing strategy whereby a portion of the value created for customers is recouped by the company.[1]

In other words, companies receive value from suppliers, and they compensate those suppliers by returning a portion of the value created. In turn, they create value for *their* customers and are able to extract some value in return, which (hopefully) allows them to generate positive *net* value for their owners. As we've discussed previously, too many companies allow their customers to keep more than a fair share of the value created. And worse, those customers are often unaware of and therefore underappreciate the actual value created by their purchase of the supplier's product. Dollarization is the bridge that enables a company to link and leverage the value it creates and the value it extracts (see Figure 3.1).

AFTER THE COST CUTTING IS DONE

Organizations have a limited number of tools available to drive profit expansion. Cost cutting and productivity enhancements are important weapons, and good companies must be relentless in their continuing management of costs and productivity, but these approaches are inherently limited. A company that cuts its costs 5 percent every year will ultimately approach zero cost. It

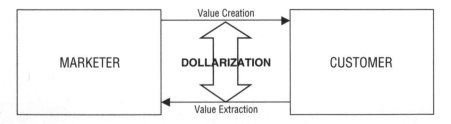

FIGURE 3.1   Dollarization Enables a Company to Equitably Extract Some of the Customer Value It Creates

will hit the bone, where no more fat can be excised. Meanwhile, emerging globalism is robbing many traditional market leaders of the pricing power on which they once relied for sustaining profitability.

Timothy Aeppel of the *Wall Street Journal* observes: "Many companies have already jumped through hoops to cut costs and boost productivity. So now they need to find ways to wring more money from their customers."[2]

Once cost cutting reaches diminishing returns, companies must look for ways to grow the top line, through expanded sales, higher prices, or both. The traditional growth levers available to marketers include:

- *Earning more share of volume* or more "share of wallet" from existing customers. (Companies can also grow when their customers sell more, but this derived demand is not directly within the marketer's span of control.)
- Add *new customers* in current markets.
- Introduce *new products or services* to existing or new customers.
- Enter *new geographies*.
- Sell *new applications or uses* for existing products/services.
- Enter *new market segments*.
- Raise *prices*.
- Reduce controllable customer *attrition*.

Throughout this book, we demonstrate how dollarization can help improve the effectiveness of each of these marketing endeavors.

VALUE OF COMPETING FOR INCHES

Managers may salivate at the opportunity to earn outrageously high prices when delivering exceptional value to customers. However, in reality, the power of dollarization typically lives in the leverage of a few incremental gains. Consider how the following improvements would impact your company:

If your company has 100 salespeople and they could each win one incremental sale because of dollarization, what would that be worth to your bottom line?

_____ Total Salespeople

_____ × Incremental Wins per Salesperson

_____ × Average Annual Value per New Sale

_____ × Life of Sale (Years)

_____ = Value of Increased Sales

If your company's average gross margin increases by just 1 percent, what would that be worth?

_____ Total Sales Revenue

_____ × Increase in Margin Points

_____ = Value of Increased Margin

If you could reduce the controllable loss of business to competition by 5 percent per year, what are those rescued sales worth? (*Note:* Some attrition is uncontrollable, such as when a customer closes a plant or discontinues a product line.)

_____ Total Annual Revenues
_____ × Typical Attrition to Competition (%)
_____ × Reduction in Attrition (%)
_____ = Value of Reduced Attrition

In our experience, the economic benefit of effective dollarization is far in excess of the cost of implementation. When an organization develops the discipline to dollarize, it wins on multiple fronts. The company begins to win more of the close competitive fights that once were lost. It also grows business with existing customers through a new recognition of the economic contributions made. Importantly, overall profit margins inch upward due to smarter pricing and an increased sense of organizational confidence.

PROTECT YOUR PRICE

An important motivator for many companies that utilize dollarization is the protection of a price premium or the defense against price erosion (or both). While companies may recognize these as strategically important, it is important for all front-line sales and marketing staff to appreciate just how much profit leverage can be gained by protecting price. It is not uncommon to hear a salesperson say under marketplace duress, "The customer is demanding a 3 percent price cut. It's only 3 percent . . . I'd rather give in to that demand than risk losing the business." In reality, few customers (more precisely, few _smart_ customers) would subject themselves to switching suppliers simply to gain a few points on the price. But fearing the worst, the seller considers capitulating to the seemingly modest request for a price reduction. The following information will help put that decision in better perspective:

1. A McKinsey study of Fortune 1000 companies showed that, on average, a 1 percent price cut lowers operating earnings by 8 percent (assuming no change in volume or costs).
2. Another composite study of 500 companies across multiple industries showed the relative impact on operating income of price and three other business variables (see Figure 3.2).

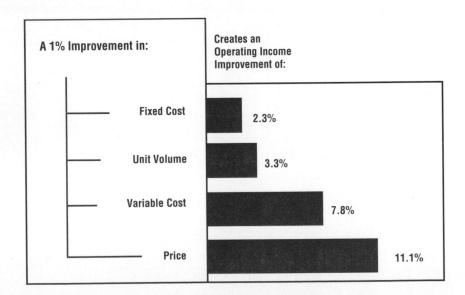

FIGURE 3.2   The Leverage of Price and Profit
Source: Michael Mara and Robert Roriello, "Managing Price, Gaining Profit," *Harvard Business Review* (September–October 1992): 85.

3. To assess the impact on your own situation, use the following formula:

$$\frac{\text{Gross Margin (\%)}}{\text{Current Gross Margin (\%)} - \text{Price Cut (\%)}} - 1 = \begin{array}{c} \text{Percentage Increase} \\ \text{in Volume Required} \\ \text{to Generate} \\ \text{the Same Total} \\ \text{Margin Dollars} \end{array}$$

So if a salesperson is considering a 3 percent price cut and the current gross margin is 40 percent, the impact is as follows:

$$\frac{0.40}{0.40 - 0.03} = 1.018; \ 1.081 - 1 = 0.081 = 8.1\%$$

This salesperson would have to gain 8.1 percent in incremental unit volume at the new reduced price in order to generate the same amount of gross margin dollars he or she was producing before the price cut.

STRATEGIC VALUE OF DOLLARIZATION

In addition to winning new sales and improving pricing, dollarization also enables the marketer to gain a deeper understanding of the customer. This understanding keeps the marketer focused on what is truly important to the customer, and helps the marketer make strategic marketing decisions—about product direction, sales approaches, pricing strategies, channel development—that are fundamentally more sound than traditional approaches.

Because assessing value in monetary terms initially appears to be such a daunting task, most firms in business markets do not even try to do it. Yet, the small but growing number of progressive firms that excel at value assessment find that the more value assessments they do, the easier they become. That is, through experience and learning, they develop this business marketing capability. They also uniformly find that value assessment provides them with superior knowledge about the marketplace that they are able to convert to superior marketplace performance.[3]

Companies that become dollarization disciples find that inside-out decision making gives way to a customer-focused mentality. Every decision that impacts the customer can be tested through a dollarization filter: How does this impact the value we create for our customers?

Chapter 4

After the Bubble Burst

As proponents of dollarization, we have been intrigued to observe the emergence of so-called tech companies as leading users of this approach to selling and marketing. The events leading up to this moment are instructive.

We have been helping companies dollarize and otherwise add discipline to their marketing activities for many years. So as with many other traditionalists, we were appalled (and sometimes amused) at the vast amount of marketing dollars shredded during the heady days of the technology bubble of 1998–2000. Driven by the seemingly endless potential of the Internet and e-commerce, businesses were expanding their information technology (IT) expenditures with no end in sight, and every tech company seemed to have the perfect solution searching for a need. Rich with initial public offering (IPO) lucre and promises of contracts from loose-spending customers, the tech world set out on a brand-building stampede like never before seen.

The zenith was perhaps the 2000 Super Bowl, where dot-com companies accounted for approximately half of the advertising time, each spending $2.2 million for 30 seconds of exposure (this stampede had inflated the price from $1.6 million a year earlier). But much of the advertising left observers wondering: What does that company sell? Why should anyone invest in its product?

In the aftermath of the bubble, after many once-promising firms and ideas went by the wayside, a new discipline seems to have emerged. Just as their stock prices have experienced a correction, their marketing and sales approaches have been corrected by market forces as well. Tech companies that once survived on the backs of dot-coms and their free-spending corporate brethren now must compete for the business of considerably fewer customers with much tighter budgets. With this realization, the techies now seem to recognize that their offerings must provide robust economic returns in order to earn consideration from prospective customers. Where hubris once was the lead selling strategy, a focus on dollarized returns is now the prominent approach.

We expect this shift was largely customer driven, as chief information officers (CIOs) around the world had lost credibility within their organizations for chasing expensive new technologies without a firm handle on their real value to the company. IT departments were sharply scrutinized at every turn, and their vendors were also put under the microscope. IT buyers demanded return on investment (ROI) analyses from suppliers, and tech companies scrambled to deliver. According to a 2001 *CIO* magazine study cited in a Cisco Systems marketing presentation, "80% of all enterprises now require some form of ROI analysis." (See Figure 4.1.)

What has emerged now is a wave of marketing claims not based in hype, but instead built on a foundation of tying technology's promise to its economic impact for the customer. A few examples, pre- and postbubble, are shown in Figures 4.2, 4.3, and 4.4.

FIGURE 4.1 Corporate IT departments are forcing technology suppliers to dollarize their offerings. "DILBERT" reprinted by permission of United Feature Syndicate, Inc.

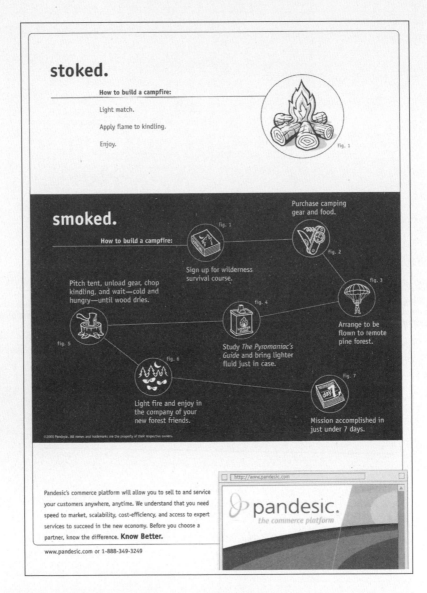

FIGURE 4.2 These ads ran in 1999–2000. They are two (of many) examples of companies that advertised poorly, and did not survive to change their ways.

FIGURE 4.2 *(Continued)*

FIGURE 4.3 These companies made their mistakes during the boom days, but today prominently feature return on investment on their websites.

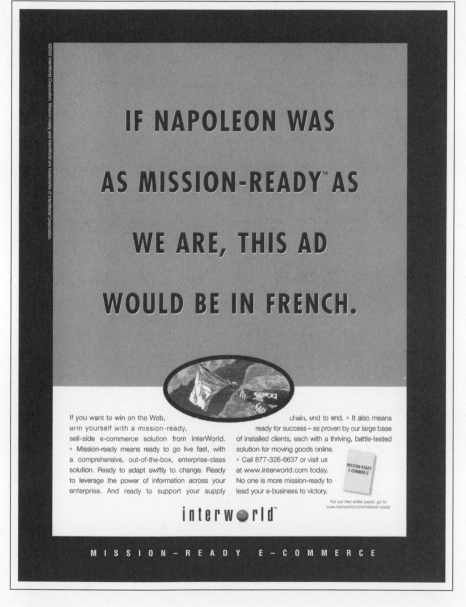

FIGURE 4.3 *(Continued)*

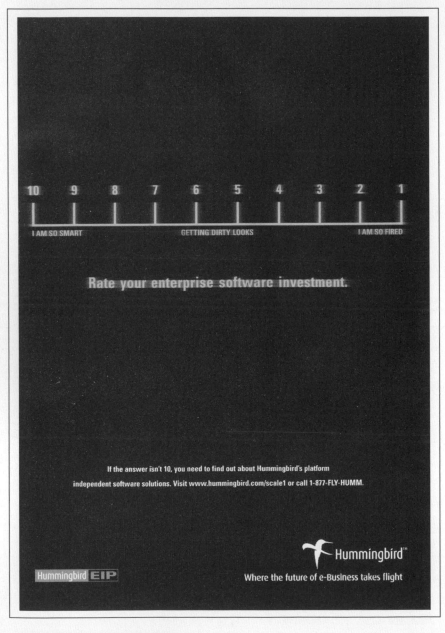

FIGURE 4.3 *(Continued)*

THE OBSESSIVE GOAL OF ALMOST
ANY B2B NET MARKETPLACE IS TO
GET OFF THE GROUND. FLYING, IT'S
ASSUMED, WILL FOLLOW NATURALLY.

The first step to B2B e-commerce is to aggregate
content. Then it's up, up and away, right? Wrong.
Emerging as a winner depends on much more. You
need a plan to manage content so that suppliers
can make constant updates and marketplaces have
a structure all B2B players will embrace. Requisite
Technology makes it possible. We have the people,
the process and the patents to prove it, from catalog
transformation services to tools for maintaining
interoperable e-content. Simply put, without a complete e-content solution, a net marketplace won't fly.
For additional rules to help B2B e-commerce take
off, visit us at www.requisiterules.com.

requisitetechnology™

E-CONTENT SOLUTIONS THAT POWER B2B E-COMMERCE. | www.requisite.com

FIGURE 4.3   *(Continued)*

FIGURE 4.4 Led by a relentless IBM print campaign, the postbubble technology advertising landscape is tightly focused on financial returns.

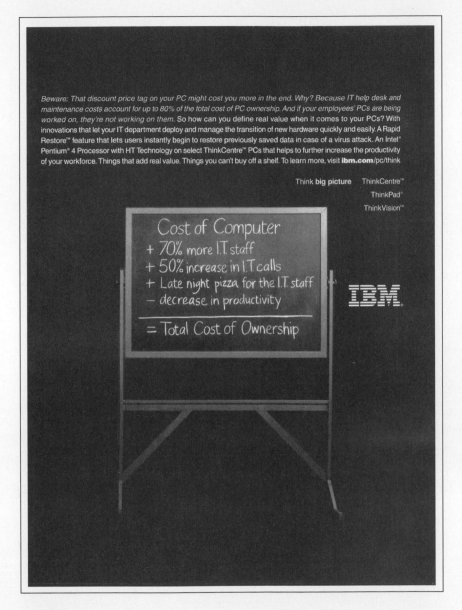

FIGURE 4.4 *(Continued)*

FIGURE 4.4 *(Continued)*

A guide to the on demand world: Hidden value

Where to find a million dollars you never knew you had.

Chances are you're sitting on some cash. Problem is, it could be anywhere. Behind your servers. Stuck in a silo. Buried in your processes. Or underneath Mike in marketing. You may not have it in your sights, but one thing is for sure, it's there. So how do you find it?

IBM business consultants help you root out bottlenecks, turf wars and cultural ruts and turn them into new revenue streams or avoided costs. By running at a state of über-efficiency, everything falls into place. Nothing can hide. Nothing gets mired down. And savings get tilled back in.

In a time when IT money is limited to what you can shake out of the corporate couch cushions, on demand options are plentiful. Like outsourcing. Grid computing. Pay-as-you-go resources. And Linux.® All efficiency boosters. All without a complete overhaul.

Can you see it? It's an on demand world. And IBM Business Consulting Services can look at your business holistically (at the macro level) and then jump in (at the micro level) to bring hidden opportunities to the surface. So you can squeeze every dollar, euro and dinar out of them. You show us the couch, we'll help show you the cash. On demand business. Get there with @ business on demand™

ibm.com/ondemand

FIGURE 4.4   *(Continued)*

FIGURE 4.4 *(Continued)*

DOLLARIZATION AND SELLING

What is a cynic? A man who knows the price of everything, and the value of nothing.

—Oscar Wilde

Early to bed, early to rise. Sell hard, and dollarize!

—Jeffrey J. Fox

Chapter 5

Dollarization and Selling Your Price

By far the most common application of dollarization we are asked about involves its use as a competitive tool in personal, face-to-face selling. Within this realm, there are many specific situations that demand dollarization. Some of the more common instances include:

- Handling a customer price objection.
- Dealing with a customer request for a price reduction.
- Escaping treatment as a commodity.

In this chapter, we review each of these with examples and illustrations.

THE PRICE OBJECTION

The price objection can come in many forms, and somewhere in the course of every sale at least one of these forms is likely to present itself. In order to buy something, customers must give up money, of which they have a limited supply. This creates tension, driven by the implicit economic reluctance to part with cash. Even a customer who trusts the seller and desires to buy the product wants to be sure of getting a good deal. In the absence of other financial information, the customer focuses on the price, which represents the imminent sacrifice of dollars.

Price objections create extraordinary angst among sellers. In fact, the very *mention* of price, by itself, gives 90 percent of all sellers the shivers. Much of this is purely psychological and fear-driven. But the fear is based in insecurity, not fact.

If the seller truly believes that his or her product is worth its price, then the burden is on the salesperson to demonstrate the price/value relationship to the customer. It is the rare customer who will accurately assess this relationship without help from the seller.

Some of the common forms of price objection that sellers hear include:

- "What's this going to cost me?"
- "Your product is expensive."
- "Your price is higher than your competitor's price."
- "I don't have the money in my budget."

To first overcome the psychological difficulties of dealing with the price objection, the seller needs to keep two simple facts in mind:

1. In most cases, the simple question "What is your price?" has no subversive intent. Usually, the customer simply wants to know the price.

2. Often, the customer is fully (or at least largely) aware of the seller's price, the customer's own budget, and the competitive price situation *before* agreeing to meet with or talk to the seller. Despite knowing all this, the customer is still willing to discuss a potential purchase. Certainly, the customer will want to negotiate to ensure he pays the best price possible. And certainly, some customers use the price objection solely as a tool to drive down the seller's price. But most customers simply want or need the seller to help them understand why they should invest in the seller's offering over other options, or why they should move budget money around to enable an investment in the seller's offering. Often this is motivated by the customer's need to make the same case internally with his or her colleagues. The customer *needs* the seller *to demonstrate the dollarized value of investing in the seller's solution.*

It is also important to understand as sellers that the price-only customer is fickle and probably not a healthy addition to the selling company's customer portfolio. Price-only customers do not merit much investment of selling resources. Guard against the price-only customer!

We have seen thousands of salespeople over the years. Many fold when a price objection is voiced by a customer, while others rise to the occasion. Two of the best we've seen handle the price objection do it quite differently. The first, a seasoned sales veteran with boundless confidence in his company's ability to create value for customers, simply responds this way:

Customer: Your prices are too high!
Salesperson: Aw, everybody says that. (*Waving his hand and continuing with his sales call without missing a beat.*)

The second salesperson is a true dollarization disciple. He handles the price objection by bringing it up long before the customer voices it (the preemptive strike is generally a sound strategy for addressing anticipated customer objections—it takes the wind out of their sails). Early in the sales process, this salesperson says,

> You need to be aware of something right from the start. When it comes time to propose a price for this program, I can guarantee we will *not* be the lowest. In fact, our price will likely be at the high end. However, as I work with you, I intend to show you how that does not matter. I will help you evaluate how my product will reduce your costs in areas other than price, so that your total cost picture will be much more attractive, even with my higher price. If that's okay with you, let's get started, okay?

By establishing this understanding at the outset, before price is even on the table, this salesperson changes the rules of the game in favor of a total dollarized value approach. If the customer disagrees, the salesperson knows to invest his selling time elsewhere.

Example 1

In some cases, the price objection results from the prospective customer's lack of familiarity with the seller's offering or the category of offering. When Riverhead Consulting, Inc.,* an inter-

---

*The name Riverhead Consulting, Inc., has been substituted to protect the confidentiality of the company discussed in this case study.

national public affairs consulting firm, presents its comprehensive solutions to corporations, the monthly retainer is often in the mid to high five figures. If the target client is accustomed to working with premier management consultants and investment bankers, those fees may come as no surprise. But for a client public affairs manager who more frequently works with state-level lobbyists and public relations firms, such fees can generate a reaction requiring the Heimlich maneuver.

For Riverhead Consulting, the value answer is a singular focus on the economic worth of the business outcomes the firm achieves for clients (see more in Chapter 12, "Dollarization and Selling Services"). Rather than slog through dozens of PowerPoint slides detailing the processes they would use to achieve the client's objectives (and more slides highlighting the highly polished and accomplished resumes of their team members), Riverhead Consulting focuses only on the client business objectives, and on the dollarized value of achieving those objectives.

When helping a food company break into the school lunch program regulated and funded by the United States Department of Agriculture (USDA), the Riverhead Consulting fee was correctly presented as the client's investment to gain access to a multimillion-dollar market. When helping a sporting goods company address a legislative trend that would effectively illegalize the client company's core products, the Riverhead Consulting fee was positioned as an investment to rescue several hundred million dollars in annual sales in dire jeopardy, and to quite possibly ensure the literal viability of the business.

In these and countless other cases, the client may still view the investment in Riverhead Consulting as significant, but due to the dollarization strategy both the buyers and sellers remain focused on the economic endgame. The client assesses the proposed fee in light of the potential return, not as a measure of billable hours. By keeping the conversation focused on the outcomes, both buyer and seller stay concentrated on the real financial business objectives rather than on the means for achieving them.

Example 2

In 1995, Master Separations,* a start-up company, introduced a breakthrough high-speed centrifuge design for the pharmaceutical and fine chemical industries. The product, branded Masterfuge, offered customers a unique set of capabilities that was unavailable in any other technology. Competing with established technologies such as filtration and conventional centrifuges, Masterfuge combined the best of each, with none of the traditional drawbacks. The design, used for separating particles in liquid drug and chemical formulations, was clever, but untested and unfamiliar to Master's target customers, the world's largest pharmaceutical and chemical manufacturers.

Master developed its pricing strategy based on early dollarization work, which showed that Masterfuge, through yield improvements and other process advantages, could produce millions of dollars in savings and other economic value for the target customers. The price, which ranged well into seven figures for larger models, was a shock at first to the prospective buyers. While intrigued by its technical promise, they were reluctant to make such a large investment in an unfamiliar technology.

In addition, Master's position as a start-up created an addi-

---

*The name Master Separations has been substituted to protect the confidentiality of the company discussed in this case study.

tional risk consideration for the potential buyers, who were generally risk-averse.

Recognizing this, Master knew that it would need to dollarize Masterfuge's performance advantages in such a way that the economic promise would overcome the perceived risk. Every Master salesperson and application specialist was trained in dollarization, and Master retained industry process consultants to help analyze each potential customer application. The economic gains produced by the dollarization models, and validated by laboratory testing, were overwhelming, with one-year paybacks not uncommon (see Figure 5.1). Through this work and through skillful risk mitigation strategies, Master was able to make early adopters out of a group of perennial conservative followers.

Unlike the preceding examples, customers in most commercial situations *are* familiar with the seller's offering, or at least with the category of offering. Here, the price objection can result either from a lack of understanding of the true value, from an institutionally mandated focus on price only, or from a misunderstanding of the real differences between the seller's offering and the competition.

In industrial and other technical selling, the specifiers of a product are often not the same people who negotiate the price for the product. As a result, the specifiers may achieve the depth of understanding required to evaluate the value of an offering, but the procurement part of the organization has only a superficial understanding (at best) and therefore puts its buying emphasis on getting the lowest price (versus the lowest actual cost or highest total return).

This condition is exacerbated by a trend championed in Detroit by U.S. carmakers (and spreading to general industry,

	Filtration	Masterfuge	SAVINGS
Total Protein Output Required (grams)	8,670	8,670	
÷ Process Yield (grams per liter)	0.51	1.26	
= Amount of Initial Lysate Required (liters)	17,000	6,880	
x Cost per Liter	$80	$80	
= Cost of Initial Lysate	$1,360,000	$550,400	$809,600
Initial Cell Lysate Required (liters)	17,000	6,880	
÷ Liters per Batch (based on fermentor size)	1,000	1,000	
= Number of Batches Required	17	7	
x Downstream Resin Loss per Batch (liters)	250	50	
x Cost per Liter of Resin	$60	$60	
= Resin Replacement Loss	$255,000	$21,000	$234,000
TOTAL SAVINGS PER YEAR			**$1,043,600**
Payback Period			**0.77 Years**

FIGURE 5.1   Sample Dollarization Analysis (Pharmaceutical Application of Masterfuge)

aerospace, and elsewhere). This trend is the *intentional* isolation of the procurement function from the other functional areas of a company. For example, it is not uncommon to find purchasing agents at large automotive companies who are rewarded based on the price concessions they can wring from suppliers. If a purchasing agent or buyer "saves" 50 cents by buying a cheaper part, but that part lives up to its cheap reputation and creates $100 in warranty problems in the finished car, the buyer still gets a bonus and bears no responsibility for the ultimate warranty costs and ultimate loss of customers.

Buyers have admitted in candid interviews that they will tell salespeople, in effect, "I know your product is better and I believe it is worth the higher price, but I won't get my bonus if I select you." In such cases, the seller must find decision makers with adequate authority to override this short-sighted incentive and do what is in the best interest of the entire company.

Anderson and Narus had this to say on the same phenomenon:

> Customers—especially those whose costs are driven by what they purchase—increasingly look to purchasing as a way to increase profits and therefore pressure suppliers to reduce prices. To persuade customers to focus on total costs rather than simply on acquisition price, a supplier must have an accurate understanding of what its customers value, and would value."[1]

When companies behave this way, the first course of action should be to attempt to get someone in the purchasing group to see that the dollarization approach could help that person gain praise in his or her organization (see Chapter 22). One approach is to lay the opportunity on the table in the hope the buyer will rise to the bait:

> Ms. Buyer, based on our preliminary evaluation and on experience with other companies in similar situations, we are fairly confident that we can save your company more than $40,000, even when you account for the higher price of our product. What I need to know is who in your company

should get credit for identifying those savings, and what do I have to do to make sure that person gets credit for the $40,000 savings?

This approach, or variations thereof, can get some reluctant buyers to open their thinking to consider that perhaps price is not the *only* consideration.

Even with approaches like this, it can be difficult to get purchasing groups to appreciate value. When the purchasing department is intractable and considers price over any other assessment of financial value, it becomes incumbent upon the seller to find influential decision makers elsewhere in the company who care about the overall economic health of the business, and not just the purchase price. Clearly, this needs to be done carefully, as narrow-minded buyers could become vindictive if their wishes are summarily dismissed. But consultative sellers must think as if they were members of the customer team. They cannot let one part of the customer organization (purchasing) force a decision that will hurt the business as a whole.

These situations often require finding a decision maker with broad enough perspective to appreciate the value that specific functional areas (i.e., purchasing) do not. Here is an effective way to approach the senior player:

Ms. Vice President, we have been working with your production and purchasing departments and have identified some problems we can help your company solve that will generate more than $40,000 in immediate savings. You have some good people in the purchasing group, and they are working hard to get the lowest price for this product. Frankly, our price is higher than the other company they are considering, but the total cost picture is better by $40,000 if you go with our solution. Would you consider evaluating this opportunity?

Also, I know the purchasing people are doing their jobs, and they may become upset if they hear that I approached you with this. How do you suggest we handle this with them?

When you have exhausted all available strategies and the buyer's focus on price continues to go beyond what is rational and reasonable, it can be useful to employ reductio ad absurdum, or reduction to the absurd. This technique can be useful, but be warned: It must be used carefully! It is often saved as a last resort, and should be delivered with good humor (and low expectations).

Consider this paraphrase of a conversation we've had with difficult buyers:

Buyer: As far as we're concerned, we will buy from whatever gear company offers the lowest price. I don't care about your supposed "advantages."

Seller: So, if you could spend nothing on this gear, you'd be happy.

Buyer: Exactly. Very happy.

Seller: Well, there *is* a way you can do that and save *all* the money you would spend on gears: Don't buy any gears.

Buyer: Excuse me?

Seller: That's right. Don't buy any. That would save your entire budget.

Buyer: Yes, it would. But our machines wouldn't run without gears.

Seller: Oh, the operation of your machines is a factor in your decision?

The conversation has now returned to the underlying reason why the customer needs to buy the seller's product. By bringing it to an absurd level, the seller has made the point that product performance and price must be considered in concert.

HONEST PRICE OBJECTIONS

As stated previously, the most common price objections are rather innocent in nature. They derive from limited customer budgets and incomplete understanding of the economic gain provided in return for the price paid. In these cases, the purpose of dollarization is to educate the customer to the quantified performance differences between available offerings and the dollarized value created by those offerings.

Example 1

Remsen Security Products* is the world's leading manufacturer of premium commercial door hardware (locks, door closers, and emergency exit devices). Remsen was facing increasing price competition from overseas players and was seeing erosion in its market share position. The company's products were technically superior to competitive products, yet customers were increasingly unable to justify paying the corresponding price premium.

Several competitive products met the minimum industry specification, which earned them the right to bid on most

---

*The name Remsen Security Products has been substituted to protect the confidentiality of the company discussed in this case study.

public projects. However, Remsen's products far exceeded the minimum requirements. Many customers, including public entities, preferred the Remsen brand, but were unable to select the higher-priced Remsen product—sometimes they were prohibited by law—when an approved lower-priced product was available.

Many loyal Remsen customers told the company that they wanted to buy the Remsen product because they were convinced of its technical superiority, but they did not have adequate information for making this case with the financial sides of their organizations.

After wrestling with this issue for years, Remsen's sales, marketing, and technical leaders set out to identify and articulate an accurate economic justification for the company's key products. This involved conducting a comprehensive marketplace study to quantify the actual costs involved in owning inferior door hardware.

Ultimately, data from nearly 200 universities, schools, hospitals, and commercial buildings (representing millions of doors) was studied to identify the frequency of maintenance required by major brands of hardware. The results enabled Remsen to predict the potential savings a facility could realize by selecting the Remsen brand over competitive alternatives.

The results of the study were designed into a PC-based calculator that enabled the Remsen sales force and channel partners (including distributors and independent agents) to calculate—with the prospective customer—the savings that would accrue by selecting Remsen hardware. They simply entered the number of doors to be equipped with the various types of hardware and the incremental investment required to purchase from Remsen, and the calculator provided a total savings estimate and a payback analysis that enabled the prospective customer to rationally evaluate the decision to invest in the premium hardware (see Table 5.1).

The dollarization calculator also provided a statistical estimate of the number of hardware failures that a customer could potentially avoid by installing Remsen's hardware. Because door hardware failures can often be directly linked to breaches in safety and security, this data enabled the customer to further assess the value of installing "the more expensive" option. (In other words, every time a lock required maintenance, there was an increased chance that that lock was not performing its intended safety and security function.)

And while it proved difficult to put a precise value on improved safety and security, the quantified difference in failure frequency made customers take notice.

Using these selling tools, Remsen was able to change the way it sold. Suddenly, higher-level decision makers (e.g., college deans instead of locksmiths) were taking an interest in the door hardware decision. Architects, who often acted as important influencers in large sales, had a new tool at their disposal to influence hardware specifications.

Another unintended outcome was the solidification of relationships with longtime customers. These customers had previously chosen Remsen based on their own intuitive assessment of the value; the formal dollarization analyses provided by Remsen gave them a strong affirmation of their prior decisions.

TABLE 5.1   Door Hardware Payback Analysis

Incremental Investment Required to Purchase Remsen Hardware	$25,000
÷Total Annual Savings	$39,887
= Payback Period	0.63 Years

Example 2

A leading automotive paints and coatings manufacturer (ABC*) was attempting to sell its outsourced paint line cleaning service to a major automaker (Acme Auto*).

The initial sales pitch promised "more efficient" use of Acme Auto manpower, "better" cleaning performance, and a series of other subjective benefits. ABC offered the service for $2,500 per paint line, which was based on an estimate of its cost to perform the service, plus a reasonable markup.

Acme Auto managers showed some initial interest, but ultimately turned down ABC's offer. They could not see the point in spending money with an outside supplier when their own people could handle the work.

Eighteen months later, ABC reinitiated conversations about outsourcing paint line cleaning for Acme. This time, ABC conducted a detailed dollarization analysis, looking at all possible cost impacts for Acme. ABC also initiated this second round of conversation with a more senior management team at Acme.

ABC offered Acme Auto management a detailed economic review of the plant's paint line cleaning (see Figure 5.2). During this review process, Acme revealed that its internal paint line cleaning costs were much higher than ABC had estimated, because the cleanings were normally performed during plant shutdowns, when union laborers received double wages. Acme came to recognize this high cost only when prompted by ABC to assess the true line-by-line expenses tied to performing this operation.

---

*The names ABC and Acme Auto have been substituted to protect the confidentiality of the companies discussed in this case study.

Paint Line Cleaning - Operating Cost Comparison	As Currently Planned	ABC Solutions
Facility Name:	ACME AUTOMOTIVE	
Proposal Date:	May 1, 2004	
Material Cost	$ –	$ –
Manpower Cost	$ 42,075.00	$ 7,341.00
Equipment Cost	$ 16,740.00	$ · 2,750.00
Product / Waste Disposal Cost	$ –	$ –
Plugged Drops and Dirty Line Cost	$ 3,824.00	$ –
Scrap Cost Associated with Dirty Lines	$ –	$ –
Additional Emergency Cost	$ –	$ –
Cost Comparison (Current vs. ABC Process)	$ 62,639.00	$ 10,091.00

FIGURE 5.2   Summary Value Analysis and Economic Return

Based on this analysis, ABC discovered that it could save Acme tens of thousands of dollars by outsourcing paint line cleaning.

ABC adjusted its selling strategy and increased its price to $7,500 per line to reflect the value it was delivering. Acme accepted the offer, and even at this new price, Acme would save more than $5,000 per line.

PRICE DOWNS AND COMMODITIZATION

Modern purchasing departments use several other strategies to get lower prices, but there are two that have become increasingly prevalent. If the previous section was about *innocent* price objections—where the customer simply needs to be educated to appreciate the true value of a product—then this section is about the *dishonest* variety.

The first customer approach is the blunt, aggressive demand for year-over-year price reductions from suppliers. This is where buyers say, in essence, "If you would like to continue supplying these products, you will have to deliver annual price reductions of X percent." Some companies are more generous, and call these reductions "productivity" gains, whereby the seller must demonstrate savings equivalent to the percentage price reduction through a combination of price cuts and other cost improvement contributions. The Supplier Cost Reduction Effort (SCORE) at Chrysler Corporation is the most famous example of this, although that program, as many do, devolved into a price-down-only contest.

The second approach is the treatment of supplier products as commodities. Some purchasing departments have designated "commodity buyers" to let the suppliers know where they stand. This is a more subtle approach because one of its intended outcomes is to put the seller on the defensive psychologically. That is, by defining the seller's product as a so-called commodity, the seller may begin to question his product differentiation and doubt the impact his offering has on the customer's business (see Chapter 17 for more on commodities).

In both cases, dollarization is a powerful tool for helping deflect these buyer behaviors. When price demands are made, the seller must be ready to counter them by detailing the economic consequences facing the buyer if the seller's product were to be replaced. When these situations arise in the course of an ongoing customer relationship, the Customer Value File (CVF—see Chapter 8 and Chapter 23) is an essential tool.

Another effective strategy is to anticipate these tactics and plan for them in advance. For example, when it is expected that the customer will demand a price down, the seller can use what we call the "window of opportunity" pricing approach.

Window of Opportunity Pricing

Many customers continue to press for year-over-year price reductions. In fact, many customer purchasing people are compensated based on the year-over-year price downs they can win from suppliers.

Meanwhile, traditional price strategies are based more on the cost of manufacturing a product than on the value the product delivers to the customer.

When this occurs, the only reasonable way to maintain profitability is to squeeze cost out of your supply chain and manufacturing processes. While these are important disciplines to pursue, they are generally insufficient for keeping up with customer-driven demands.

An alternative approach is to create a multiyear price strategy based on the dollarized value generated by the product.

What follows is a simple model for new product pricing that acknowledges the reality that, over time, most products lose the competitive advantage they may have enjoyed when new. Knowing that competitive pressures will likely increase during a product's or application's lifetime, and knowing that customer price-down requests are inevitable, the manufacturer should establish the following fundamental philosophies.

- When a product or application is new and enjoys a meaningful competitive advantage, set pricing according to the product's true dollarized value and capture as much of that value as possible.

- Plan to see the price of a new product or application decline as competitors respond with viable alternatives and customers seek price reductions.

- Continuously improve the product line so that when competition begins to erode pricing, a new, better product can be introduced to reestablish the competitive advantage.

Specifically, the window of opportunity approach can be used to preemptively address customer price-down requests. The strategy calls for creating an *intentional* year-over-year price down by setting the year 1 pricing based on the dollarized value (see Figure 5.3). The price is then stepped down year after year, accomplishing four things.

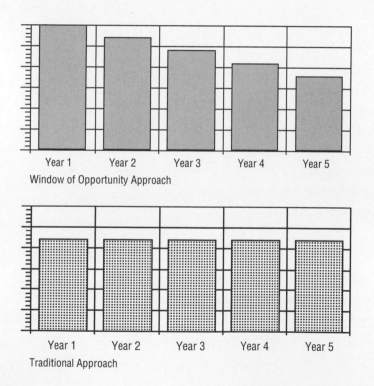

Year 1   Year 2   Year 3   Year 4   Year 5
Window of Opportunity Approach

Year 1   Year 2   Year 3   Year 4   Year 5
Traditional Approach

FIGURE 5.3 Window of Opportunity Pricing: Illustrated

1. The initial price reflects the value created by the seller, and rewards the seller for that value. This also allows the seller to recoup some of the up-front selling and start-up costs.

2. The buyer gets credit for annual price reductions.

3. By seeing price reductions planned for the coming years, a buyer is more likely to accept a first-year price that might be otherwise considered too high.

4. The seller's price gets closer to market pricing over time, reducing the customer's incentive (and leverage) to switch suppliers for a lower price.

Chapter 6

Dollarization and Selling Something New

One of the more difficult challenges in selling is persuading customers to purchase a new product or service when they are currently satisfied using an established, entrenched technology or methodology. Even when a new product entices the customer with great promise, the risk of failure often scuttles the potential purchase. Yet innovation and new products are the lifeblood of growing companies, so success in this selling arena is critical. Dollarization can help move even the most reluctant customer to action. (*Note:* New product pricing is addressed separately in Chapter 14.)

The challenge when selling a new concept is to demonstrate to the prospective customer that, despite the apparent risks of leaving behind the tried-and-true, the new product will produce a financial return so attractive that the customer would be committing management malpractice by not—at a minimum—testing the new product. (Nearly all new products or methods will be tested or validated in some form before any significant commitments are made by the customer.)

The financial argument plays out as follows: The customer

considers the "net value" delivered by a product or service, which can be expressed as:

$$\text{Net Value} = (\text{Dollarized Value} - \text{Cost of Risk}) - \text{Price}$$

In other words, to understand the true net value of a product offering, the customer must assess the dollarized value the offering is expected to create, adjust that for any perceived risk (the chance that the offering might fail to perform as promised), and then subtract the purchase price.

When comparing two established products, the customer analysis is simplified, because the cost of risk associated with the two established products, due to experience, is comparable and perhaps even negligible. However, when a customer is considering a new, unproven product or service, the net value for the new offering can be greatly impacted by the customer's perceived cost of risk for the new product.

In order to move the customer to buy, the new product seller must demonstrate that:

$$\text{Net Value}_{\text{New Product}} > \text{Net Value}_{\text{Old Product}}$$

To accomplish this, the seller's missions are: (1) to articulate the dollarized value of the new offering, (2) to develop and execute a strategy for minimizing the customer's perceived cost of risk, and (3) to present a price that makes financial sense given the other variables involved.

Much of this book addresses the first point, and we provide some new product dollarization examples later in this chapter. But first, let's address the second point: the mitigation of the customer's perceived cost of risk.

We have observed two key challenges in dealing with the

customer's perceived cost of risk. First, the customer is frequently comfortable and complacent with the current product or service. Even if the current offering carries with it certain problems or compromises, customers often are blissfully unaware of the solvable problems with which they are living and unaware of what those problems are actually costing their companies. Second, because newness brings with it a vacuum of experience or reviewable data, buying companies tend to overestimate the risk of switching to something new. (How many times have you heard a manager say, "The devil you know is better than the devil you don't"?)

To illustrate the "customer complacency" point, several years ago we visited a large automotive axle manufacturer with a client salesperson. The seller's objective was to review his line of hydraulic sealants with the customer in order to discover potential applications. (Hydraulic sealants are used to reduce leakage of oil and other fluids from working equipment.) Upon arrival, the seller and customer engaged in preliminary conversation, with the seller asking to see the customer's worst leakage problems. The customer replied (sincerely) that he "didn't have any leakage problems." The seller was incredulous, but calmly suggested that they do a plant walk-through to see if they might discover any opportunities to work together. The customer agreed, and then suggested that we each put on a pair of rubber boots to protect our shoes! The plant floor was covered with oils, hydraulic fluids, and other leaks, but those were "normal" leaks in the customer's mind. The customer had learned to live with the solvable problem and didn't know there was a way to eliminate those leaks. Nor did the customer know the dollarized value of eliminating the leaks; he did not know what it was costing his company to go without the solution.

This lack of awareness or conditioned acceptance of problems is a challenge for the new product seller because the adoption of a new product by a business typically requires some investment in manpower and other resources to validate and convert to the new product. If there is no current awareness, let alone dissatisfaction, there is little incentive for the customer to make such investments. Thus, the seller must provide a wake-up call to get the customer's attention. An effective means for doing so is to illustrate the dollarized costs of continuing with the old product. Upon learning that it is costing the department $250,000 a year by not switching to a new technology, a customer will generally be more receptive to the prospect of fully vetting that technology. Once the customer further evaluates the new product he or she achieves a better understanding of the true risks involved, and a higher level of confidence in the true dollarized value.

If, on the other hand, the new product seller simply promotes the technical features and other benefits of the product, without converting those benefits to dollars, the customer is less likely to invest in an evaluation, and therefore remains saddled with a higher perceived cost of risk.

One of the selling strategies that we have found to be successful in these situations involves three steps:

1. The seller works with the customer to generate a preliminary understanding of the new product's benefits and applicability to the customer's situation.

2. The seller works with the customer to conduct a pro forma dollarization analysis. This analysis is typically based largely on the seller's own background data.

3. The seller asks the customer for a conditional buying commitment, for example:

"As we agreed, this widget could save your company more than $50,000 per year. If it performs as promised when tested, is there any other reason that would prohibit you from going forward with it?"

This approach works on several levels. First, it acknowledges the customer's need to test and validate the promise of the new, unproven product. Second, it puts the burden on the seller to prove the preliminary claims made about the product's performance. This creates a feeling of comfort for the customer. Third, it firmly puts the decision in financial terms: In order to save $50,000 per month, the customer must test the product. This makes the testing more likely to proceed in a timely manner. Fourth, the "Is there anything else?" question prompts the customer to verbalize any other hidden objections or roadblocks. And finally, once these are cleared up, the decision criteria are clearly established: If the product does indeed test as promised, the customer has committed to move ahead.

In our experience, unless there is a legitimate misunderstanding between the buyer and seller about the compatibility or applicability (or both) of the new product, this approach significantly increases the odds that the product will be tested and will perform acceptably for the customer. Testing the product greatly diminishes the perceived cost of risk, allowing the dollarized value to stand on its own.

CASE HISTORIES

The following case histories demonstrate how dollarization can pave the way for new product success.

| GLADSTONE PIPE COATINGS | | **Ultra vs. MaxBond Pipe Coating** |
| | | Economic Impact Analysis for Northern Pipeline Projects |

Project Profile

| Enter More Project Details | View Detailed Calculations | Review Cost Comparisons |
| Go to HELP Page | Enter Other Project Costs | Print Detailed Report |

Customer Name:	Vertigo Pipelines
Contact Name:	David Torrey
Project Name:	Mica Ridge
Date:	18-Jan-99

Major Project Inputs

Select Pipe Diameter (inches)	30 inches
Enter Total Pipeline Length (Kilometers)	50 KM
Enter Percentage of Route Requiring Mechanical Protection	40%
Select MaxBond Coating Thickness	14 mil
Enter Joint Length (meters)	20 Meters

Investment Summary

Incremental Investment In Ultra Pipe Coating	$194,500
Net Savings with Ultra	$243,467
Return On Investment	125%

FIGURE 6.1   The main screen on the Gladstone calculator captures key project identifiers and the basic project variables that are essential to completing the core analysis. Just by completing this screen, the customer gets a very preliminary view of Ultra's economic impact on the customer's project.

Gladstone Pipe Coatings

Gladstone Pipe Coatings* is a company that specializes in applying protective coatings to pipes used in the construction of petroleum pipelines. Most of these pipelines are installed in the Canadian and arctic wilderness, where environmental conditions are quite severe. The coatings provide many protective functions, the primary one being the safeguarding of the installed steel pipe against corrosion. Given the volume of oil trav-

---

*The name Gladstone Pipe Coatings has been substituted to protect the confidentiality of the company discussed in this case study.

Detailed Project Inputs

ENTER DETAILED PROJECT VARIABLES BELOW	Return to Major Inputs	View Detailed Calculations	Review Cost Comparisons
DEFINITIONS are provided on the HELP PAGE.	Go to HELP Page	Enter Other Project Costs	Print Detailed Report

	CHOOSE Baseline or Your Data	YOUR DATA	BASELINE DATA
Percentage Reduction of Mechanical Protection Allowed by Using Ultra Coating	Enter Your Own Data	15%	20%
Coating Pricing per Meter for MaxBond	Enter Your Own Data	$24.45	$25.77
Coating Pricing per Meter for Ultra	Use Baseline Data		$28.34
Number of Joints Coated per Day	Enter Your Own Data	160	140
Daily Crew Cost for MaxBond Joint Coating	Use Baseline Data		$9,000

FIGURE 6.2 In order to conduct a more detailed analysis, the customer can review the Detailed Project Inputs screen, which lists nearly 40 variables. Gladstone's third-party engineering study provides baseline data for typical pipeline projects, but the tool also permits the customer to enter project-specific data as needed. This step in the process is critical, as the customer is able to instantly and independently customize the analysis with internal data, and not rely solely on the supplier's numbers. Importantly, the tool also allows the customer to review the detailed calculations underpinning each analysis. This is an important step in building credibility with the customer.

eling through these often remote pipelines, the impact of a corrosion-induced leak can be catastrophic.

Gladstone's biggest-selling product was the industry standard MaxBond coating, which had achieved great acceptance among pipeline companies. (MaxBond was also manufactured by most other coatings companies.) As a market leader, Gladstone strived to advance the state of pipe coating technology, and it believed it had succeeded in doing so with its new Ultra Coating. Ultra held several performance advantages over MaxBond, and was priced at least 10 percent higher than

Comparison of Total Installed Coating-Related Costs

Cost Comparison by Category	Return to Major Inputs Go to HELP Page	View Detailed Calculations Enter Other Project Costs	Enter More Project Detail Print Detailed Report
	MaxBond	**Ultra**	**SAVINGS**
Coating Application	$1,222,500	$1,417,000	–$194,500
Weld Joint Coating Costs	$240,625	$348,750	–$108,125
Coating Repair Costs	$210,000	$31,000	$179,000
Mechanical Protection Costs	$1,200,000	$1,020,000	$180,000
Bending Costs	$20,000	$0	$20,000
Trenching Costs	$35,180	$29,903	$5,277
Cathodic Protection Costs	$125,000	$118,750	$6,250
Lower-In & Backfill Cost	$1,670,350	$1,647,573	$22,778
Supervision, Service & Overhead Costs	$9,037,500	$9,001,350	$36,150
HDD/Bore Coating Costs	$225,488	$128,850	$96,638
Other Project Costs (User entered)	$0	$0	$0
= TOTAL COSTS FOR COMPARISON	**$13,986,643**	**$13,743,176**	**$243,467**

FIGURE 6.3   This screen summarizes the dollarized results for the major cost differences. The customer can also input other cost areas not considered by Gladstone (positive or negative), and can print a detailed report to share internally with all decision makers.

MaxBond. On a typical pipeline construction project (25+ kilometers), that price differential could amount to tens or even hundreds of thousands of dollars.

Meanwhile, the target customers for Ultra were much like the axle company noted earlier. They were comfortable with MaxBond and had no major problems with its continued use as the industry standard. The argument for trying a new coating technology would need to be very compelling indeed.

Gladstone knew that Ultra's technical advantages were clear, but they consisted of many different incremental performance advantages, none of which by itself qualified as a game changer. But as a whole, Gladstone believed Ultra was a significant improvement over MaxBond for certain types of pipeline installation, particularly in remote regions with abrasive, rocky soils.

The first challenge Gladstone faced was breaking through to an industry that was historically skeptical about new technology. Gladstone realized it needed to achieve an acceptable level of credibility for the new coating, and to develop a sufficiently compelling economic story to persuade key customers to test, validate, and certify the new coating.

As part of Gladstone's marketing strategy, it commissioned a detailed engineering and cost study by a respected pipeline engineering firm, which validated and detailed the many benefits offered by Ultra. Gladstone then extracted the core cost dynamics from this engineering study and built a comprehensive cost comparison tool. This analytical tool would assess all of the elements of pipeline construction that were impacted by the technical differences between MaxBond and Ultra. These analyses were distilled into a user-friendly tool (described later) that was simple enough for a Gladstone salesperson to use with a customer, yet powerful enough to withstand scrutiny from a pipeline customer's engineering team.

Because the key benefits of Ultra accrued more or less at one time (during pipeline construction), the presentation of the final dollarization analysis was straightforward. The calculator main screen (see Figure 6.1) summarized the incremental investment required to go with Ultra versus MaxBond, and the construction savings that would be realized by making that shift. A simple return on investment calculation demonstrates the customer's return on the incremental investment to use Ultra. Figures 6.2 and 6.3 showed more detailed analysis and summary screens.

Master Separations

In Chapter 5, we discuss how Master Separations used dollarization to overcome initial price resistance when launching its revolutionary Masterfuge separation system. The system, used to separate submicron particles (smaller than the point of a pencil) in pharmaceutical and chemical formulations, was unlike any established technology. The system was intended to replace conventional technologies that sold for a fraction of the Masterfuge price.

Master utilized a disciplined approach during its launch. Nearly every piece of its attack plan was designed to reduce the customers' perception of risk and to develop detailed, dollarized business cases with prospective customers. Some of the key activities supporting the launch included:

- The marketing team developed case histories describing the key benefits delivered to other early adopter customers (see Figure 6.4). These were used to demonstrate that other companies were using Masterfuge (which helped in risk mitigation) and to demonstrate the broad capabilities the system offered, including the financial benefits.
- The company developed a scaled-down version of the Masterfuge system for laboratory testing. This enabled customers to gauge potential performance and to begin estimating the parameters that would underpin the dollarization analysis. The lab-scale system also became a tool for customers to test other product processes, which helped seed future Master sales.
- Master employed several highly competent technical experts, and it retained industry specialists to help complete thorough process reviews with potential customers. This helped identify potential issues and areas of cost impact. It also often identified benefits that were previously overlooked.

MASTER Separations

Successful Clarification of Viscous Latex Polymer

▼ Achieved difficult viscous separation ▼ Eliminated filter media, labor and disposal costs
▼ Annual Savings: $900,000

Overview:

After two years of trying to optimize its cartridge filtration method, a film manufacturer was able to clarify a viscous polymer material using Masterfuge. MASTER enabled the customer to perform a separation that was previously impossible, while also eliminating many of the costs associated with filtration. Annual savings totaled more than $900,000.

Prior Situation

A film manufacturer had been using filtration techniques to clarify one of the polymers used in the production of photographic film. The company spent over 2 years trying to optimize the filtration process, but faced difficult barriers. Essentially, a small fraction of semi-congealed solids would collect and blind the filter cartridge prematurely, resulting in frequent filter changes. Meanwhile, each filter change meant that entrained product was lost to disposal. In all, 3% of the product was lost with the spent filter cartridges. Additionally, the cost of disposal itself represented a significant and escalating concern.

The MASTER Solution

The Masterfuge is especially suited for viscous chemical applications containing "sticky" semi-solids or globules which "blind" filters. The Masterfuge enabled this customer to accomplish its clarification step successfully while eliminating virtually all of the costs associated with filtration (e.g. filter replacement costs, labor costs). Masterfuge was able to produce a dry cake discharge, eliminating much of the product loss that resulted with the entrained product in the cartridge. The resulting recovery of lost product produced a 3% yield improvement for the customer.

Additionally, MASTER configured the Masterfuge system to provide the customer a safe explosion-proof process. The elimination of clogged filter cartridges also enabled the customer to eliminate a waste disposal problem.

Investment Return Analysis

	Prior Situation	MASTER	Savings
Initial Batch Size (l)	8,000	8,000	
x Cost per Liter	$12.50	$12.50	
= Cost of Initial Batch	$100,000	$100,000	
x Yield Loss	3%	0%	
= Value of Yield Loss per Batch	$3,000	$0	$3,000
Number of Filter Cartridges per Batch	200	0	
x Cost per Cartridge	$28	NA	
= Total Cartridge Costs	$5,600	0	$5,600
Filter Change Labor Hours per Batch	8	0	
x Cost per Labor Hour	$50	NA	
= Filter Change Labor Costs	$400	0	$400
Total Savings per Batch			$9,000
x Batches per Year			100
= TOTAL SAVINGS			$900,000

OTHER SAVINGS CATEGORIES: Waste disposal costs.

FIGURE 6.4 Master Separations Application Case History

	Current Method	Master	SAVINGS
Initial Batch Size (liters)	25,000	25,000	—
X Cost per Liter	$3	$3	—
= Cost of Initial Batch	$75,000	$75,000	—
X Yield Loss	5%	0%	5%
= Lost Yield Cost	$3,750	0	$3,750
+ Drying Process Costs	$5,000	$1,500	$3,500
= SAVINGS PER BATCH			$7,250
X BATCHES PER YEAR			200
= SAVINGS PER YEAR			$1,450,000
Payback Period			0.53 Years

FIGURE 6.5   Sample Dollarization Analysis

- The cornerstone of the final sales proposal was a detailed dollarization analysis to assess the complete economic impact, including payback analysis for the new Masterfuge system (see Figure 6.5). Customer champions worked hand in hand with the Masterfuge team in the development of these analyses.

Chapter 7

Shortening the Sales Cycle

Aside from the occasional "one-call close," most sales unnecessarily take too long to consummate. CEOs and sales vice presidents fret daily about the inability of their salespeople to close deals. All too often, management, when asked, "What is your average sales cycle?" will answer with a specific time frame that is mistakenly assumed to be a fact of their business life. Time and time again, companies are able to win customer interest, move to proposal stage, but then wait for the "yes" to arrive. In some cases, decisions are driven by the customer's clock or calendar, which forces a finite end (such as the opening of a new factory or the launch of a new product). But for those situations when the seller is trying to sell something and the timing of the customer decision is discretionary, steps must be taken to move the customer to a decision.

The risks of customer purchase delay are many. Each day that passes without a decision provides a window for competitors to enter or to sharpen their offerings (or both). Each passing day also presents a chance that the customer's circumstances might change and the need for the seller's product or service might diminish or disappear. A more insidious problem with the passing of time is that the delay creates doubt in the seller's mind, and weakens resistance to customer price-down demands and other requested concessions.

In many cases, complex purchase decisions do indeed take time, and there is little the seller can do to alter the natural course of events within the customer organization. Information must be shared, testing must be completed, teams must be assembled, and bosses must be briefed. In some cases, testing mandates by regulatory agencies such as the Federal Aviation Administration (FAA) or Food and Drug Administration (FDA) create extended delays. But more often, the long sales cycle is a self-perpetuating myth. The seller believes the sale will take months to close, and therefore does not take steps to make it happen otherwise.

There are many root causes to this phenomenon. Many relate to salesperson inefficiency: Often with the very best intentions, salespeople spread themselves too thin, calling on as many customers as they can. They mistakenly believe it is their duty to serve all customers in their appointed territories. This leaves too little focused time to push each deal to a conclusion. Salespeople also fail to properly target or adequately qualify their prospects, which means they waste time and resources chasing deals with low inherent probability of success. Fortunately, these are issues that can be remedied with training, coaching, and hard work.

Other causes relate to the reality of modern corporate life. Record-high productivity statistics confirm what we already know: Company managers are doing more and more with fewer and fewer people. If you consider that most significant purchases involve up to 10 decision makers or decision influencers, and that each of those 10 busy people is burdened with a few additional tasks each and every year, it is no wonder that many consensus-driven decisions grind slowly or to a halt.

In these circumstances, dollarization can help. Dollarization *does* shorten the sales cycle.

There are three requirements to get a business to accelerate its decision-making process on a purchase:

1. *Dollarize.* The seller must present a compelling dollarized financial story. This changes the way the customer views the decision. Rather than another buying decision, the customer sees an opportunity to make money, to save money, or to stop losing money.

   The presentation of a dollarized economic reason for moving ahead with a purchase decision can distinguish an offering and place it in a unique light. Rather than being relegated as another routine decision, the dollarized story alerts the customer to the financial impact of making, or not making, a decision to move forward.

2. *Make someone a hero.* An important step in using dollarization in any customer situation is to earn the trust of one or more of the players on the customer side. You must help them understand that your dollarization approach is intended not as a selling ploy, but as a tool to make sure the customer is making a valid business decision. You also want your customer contact to understand that the glory is all hers. If you discover that your solution can save the customer $1 million, you want your contact to be dreaming of the recognition she will receive for delivering that $1 million to the company coffers. As a salesperson, you don't want the credit or a plaque on the wall; you simply want the customer to say yes. Let the customer take the credit, and do what it takes to make that happen.

3. *Create a sense of urgency.* Whether or not you are able to develop a partner on the customer side, the words used in

presenting the dollarized case must be chosen very carefully if you hope to move the purchase decision forward. For example, after completing a dollarized assessment, there are many ways to summarize the findings, but those words can have very different effects on your customer.

In order to put this topic in context, it is helpful to consider the way people think about emergency medicine versus preventive medicine. Even though we recognize the importance of preventive medicine, there is generally no urgency tied to it. It is easy, for example, to postpone exercise or a cholesterol test. However, when faced with an injury or other acute medical issue, we understand and act on the need for immediate treatment.

Customers tend to think and act the same way. Customers are more inclined to replace a defective windshield wiper when it is pouring rain than when the sun is shining. For example, we have observed that telling a customer that he "could save $XX by investing in product Y" is interesting to the customer, but is seen as somewhat remote and passive. Likewise, phrases such as "cost reduction" and "revenue improvement" are promises that do not quite grab the customer by the throat. However, if the seller tells the same customer that he "can *stop losing* $XX," suddenly he gets the customer's attention. Like the emergency room patient, the customer suddenly and clearly sees the need for action.

This use of language and presentation of the dollarized value story can be taken a step further to accelerate the sales cycle. When timing is an issue, we recommend presenting the financial argument in a time-based format. For example, if your solution is worth $100,000 to a customer, you might state the value in the following way: "Mr. Customer, as we agreed, this problem is costing your company $100,000 per year. Every week that passes means another $2,000 goes down the drain. If we wait until next month, you will lose another $8,000. What can we do to help stop these losses now?"

CASE HISTORIES

The following case study illustrates how dollarization can be used to manage and shorten the sales cycle.

Aloft Aircraft Bearings

The Wayfarer Company* was a leading supplier of precision bearings for the industrial, automotive, and aerospace industries. Wayfarer's aerospace group had developed a new bearing, called Aloft, to replace conventional bearings on the wing flaps of large commercial jetliners. The new bearing was extremely resistant to corrosion, and in laboratory testing it outlived the conventional bearing almost infinitely.

The company had introduced pricing to the market that was four to five times higher than the conventional bearings, and this premium created resistance among the airline decision makers. Even if they believed in the technical promise of the new product (which they generally did), the higher price point gave them great pause. Therefore, Wayfarer's first challenge was to demonstrate that the new bearing was a bargain even at the higher price.

---

*The name Wayfarer Company has been substituted to protect the confidentiality of the company discussed in this case study.

In addition, Wayfarer recognized that competitors were preparing to enter the market with similar technology several months down the road. Fast penetration would be critical to gaining market share and establishing a platform for long-term success.

To overcome these challenges, Wayfarer set out to develop a dollarization analysis to help airlines understand the cost impacts of converting to the new corrosion-resistant bearings.

The original impetus for the new product was premature failures in the conventional bearings. These bearings were made of steel and were largely exposed to the elements on the underside of an aircraft wing. Each time a plane ascends and descends, the environmental conditions change, creating condensation and exposure to moisture. Over time, the conventional bearings would corrode and, if the corrosion was not caught during routine maintenance, could freeze up, thus limiting the motion of a wing flap. When discovered, this condition would force an emergency maintenance event that could result in flight delays and cancellations. (It is important to note that passenger safety was not an issue, as there was sufficient redundancy built into the system to prevent such risk.)

Through conversations with airline maintenance engineers and other industry experts, Wayfarer learned that each canceled flight typically cost an airline a minimum of $30,000 (in lost revenues, labor costs, passenger compensation, rebooking costs, and so on). Wayfarer also learned that a typical maintenance event would take a plane out of service for roughly 24 hours. A single daylong event would result in a major disruption, with multiple canceled flights, complications with connecting flights, and other downstream disruptions.

Faced with interested but unmoving customers, Wayfarer developed a detailed analytical tool that enabled the customer to calculate the cost impacts of these and other related consequences (see Figure 7.1).

Number of Bearing Replacements Avoided Due to Aloft		
Frequency of Unplanned Bearing Replacement (per plane per year)		0.2
x Number of Planes		90
= Annual Bearing Replacements		18
x Percentage of Replacements Eliminated by Aloft		**85%**
= Annual Bearing Replacements Avoided		15
Flight Interruption Cost per Unplanned Replacement		
Total Time Out of Service (hours) per Bearing Replacement		24
x Average Aircraft Utilization*		42%
= Lost Flight Time (hours)		10
÷ Average Length per Flight (hours)		3
= Canceled Flights per Unplanned Replacement		3.33
x Cost per Canceled Flight		$30,000
= Cost per Unplanned Bearing Replacement	$	100,000
x Annual Bearing Replacements Avoided		15
= Annual Flight Interruption Cost Savings	$	1,530,000
Cost to Replace Conventional Bearings		
Labor Hours per Bearing Replacement		**3**
x Cost per Labor Hour	$	**125**
= Labor Cost per Bearing Replacement	$	375
+ Bearing Purchase Cost per Replacement	$	**475**
= TOTAL Replacement Cost	$	850
x Annual Bearing Replacements Saved		15
= Bearing Replacement Savings	$	13,005
Cost of Damage to Other Components (e.g., tracks, actuators)		
= Annual Damage to Other Components due to Bearing Failure	$	**45,000**
TOTAL COST SAVINGS FROM REDUCED BEARING FAILURES		
= Annual Cost for Unplanned Replacements	$	1,588,005
x Useful Life of Aloft Bearings (years)		6
= TOTAL VALUE OVER LIFE OF BEARINGS		**$9,528,030**

FIGURE 7.1 Wayfarer Company's Aloft Bearings: Unplanned Maintenance Savings Analysis

The summary product of this analysis (shown in Figure 7.2) clearly states the investment required by the customer (the purchase price plus installation costs) and the total savings generated by converting problematic old-style bearings to the new corrosion-resistant style. This analysis in itself typically yielded a very robust return on investment, which was important for

Scenario 1: Hot Spot Replacement Only		
Total Cost to Install Aloft Bearings	$	621,000
Savings Generated by Eliminating Bearing Failure	$	9,528,030
Net Savings	**$**	**8,907,030**
Return on Investment		1,434%
Savings per Month	$	123,709

FIGURE 7.2   Aloft Data Summary and Investment Analysis

distinguishing the bearing project from the many other maintenance projects on an airline's docket. But the calculation that
became the cornerstone of Wayfarer's selling strategy was the
savings per month figure, which represents the total lifetime
savings divided by the projected useful life of the product. In
selling the project, the sales team and the internal champions
at the airline had a nice clean headline on which to hang their
hats: "Every month we delay action is costing more than 120
thousand dollars! Every day costs us 4 thousand dollars to go
without this new bearing!"

The result was an elevated level of urgency for Aloft projects
within airlines, and a dramatic shortening of the selling cycle.

Chapter 8

Dollarization to Protect and Keep Business

Throughout this book and in business practice, the majority of dollarization discussions tend to focus on forward-facing, on-the-offense sales and marketing situations. Whether justifying a price for a new project, winning a competitive battle, or setting a price for a new product, most marketers apply dollarization to help *get* new business. However, dollarization can be equally useful in *protecting and keeping* existing business.

THE PERILS OF POOR BUSINESS PROTECTION

The importance of keeping current business may seem self-evident. But in general, sellers and marketers spend most of their energy on gaining new business at the expense of minding what they have already won. Managers seem to be aware that getting new customers is a much more costly endeavor than keeping customers, yet they take few proactive selling steps to prevent customer loss. There are specific risks posed by taking the current book of business for granted.

Lost Revenue

If an existing customer decides to abandon the seller entirely, or simply takes away a piece of business here or there, the implications for the seller can be significant. Consider a salesperson with a growth target of 10 percent and a sales base of $100,000. This salesperson must sell an incremental $10,000 in new business to meet this target. Now consider the impact of losing an existing customer worth $5,000. The salesperson still must reach $110,000 in total sales to hit his target, but now he is starting from a base of $95,000 rather than $100,000. The salesperson would now have to close $15,000 in new business, which represents a 50 percent increase from the original task.

In addition, when the selling company is forced to replace lost business, it faces incremental costs associated with the acquisition of new business (selling costs, credit checks, quality reviews and other customer due diligence, start-up costs, etc.). These costs are avoided when business is protected in the first place.

Lost Leverage

Even when a company does a good job servicing an existing customer, there are risks when the company does not continue to sell and reinforce the value of that ongoing support. Aggressive customers will take advantage of this by pushing for concessions after the initial agreement is in place. A common industry practice is for purchasing departments to demand price downs from their supply base during the second, third, and subsequent years of an agreement. Because these initiatives are often driven by purchasing people who do not see the broad scope of the day-to-day relationship, the seller lands in a price battle with little perceived leverage.

A related risk is described by Harry Beckwith in *Selling the Invisible*.[1] Each day, small mistakes by the selling organization can create a "deficit" in the relationship with the customer. For example, a phone call that is not promptly returned quietly creates animus in the customer. A form letter from the seller's accounts receivable department may send a bad signal. Over time, this deficit builds, and the seller is oblivious.

Lost Opportunity

A company that does a great job servicing and supplying an existing customer should by all rights be earning a chance to win additional new business with that customer. Companies talk about how it is more efficient to "up-sell" or "cross-sell" additional products to an existing customer than to go out and find a new customer. But in their fervor to up-sell and cross-sell, they overlook the importance of "back-selling." Because the seller does not adequately communicate the success of the base relationship, the targets of the new business push within the same customer underappreciate the new offering.

Lost People

People change jobs every day, yet sellers often rely on a relationship with a single customer contact to protect their position. If that contact were to move, quit, be fired, or even become ill, the seller's livelihood could suddenly be at risk. Likewise, companies often depend on the relationship of a single salesperson to protect a large piece of the company's business, even though that salesperson could give notice without warning, thus putting the business at risk.

CUSTOMER VALUE FILE

An effective strategy for blunting these risks is to proactively document and communicate the value the customer receives from the ongoing relationship. A tool we call the Customer Value File (CVF) is an effective means for organizing and documenting this information.

Customer Value File (CVF)   A comprehensive report detailing the economic value and other benefits a customer receives as a result of its business relationship with a supplier.

A Customer Value File is a detailed, dollarized summary of all the benefits, services, and investments that a company provides to its customers above and beyond its core product or service offering. Much of the value firms provide to their customers is not apparent and goes unrecognized or underappreciated. A key purpose of the CVF is to make customers aware of the comprehensive investment made on their behalf, and to help quantify the value generated by that investment. In a professional fashion, the CVF presents the customer an *accurate economic rationale for doing business with the supplier*. It endorses and supports a partnership relationship with the customer, and it reinforces the customer's original decision to buy from the supplier.

A secondary, but sometimes equally important benefit of the CVF is that it energizes the selling organization. The simple act of documenting all the wonderful things a group provides to its customers can help put their business existence in better perspective. It generates pride and renewed confidence by virtue of shedding light on all the routine activities that add up to a highly valuable economic contribution.

There are other important reasons to use CVFs. They educate different parts of the customer organization about activities in other areas. For example, purchasing learns about what is happening in engineering, engineering learns about the supplier's support of production, and production learns about developments elsewhere. Without the CVF, the seller's accomplishments may be appreciated locally, but are not leveraged across the customer organization. The CVF protects against narrowly focused aggression by any one functional area at the customer. It also creates a more fertile environment for pursuing incremental business opportunities.

The CVF helps the seller maintain a strong position and creates a documented history with a customer. It also provides a broad perspective on the seller's total contribution for high-level customer managers, and can provide an excellent forum for strategic meetings between high-level customer and seller management. Companies wishing to establish long-term strategic projects with their key customers can be helped by demonstrating the depth of involvement already in place.

We frequently hear companies say, "If we could only get an audience with the vice president, we'd really move this project forward." The CVF is a tool for getting that audience.

Positive exposure to senior management also helps the lower-level players on the customer side look good within their organizations. If they are recognized for working with committed, value-generating suppliers, they will be more open to future work with those suppliers.

The CVF is also critical in overcoming the loss of relationships caused by personnel turnover at the customer or the selling organization. Companies face this problem every day: The primary contact at the customer truly appreciates the value and support provided by the supplier. But, unexpectedly, that customer contact is transferred to another part of the company, or leaves for a better job, or is promoted. A replacement walks in with no knowledge, or extremely limited knowledge, of the existing business relationship (except for the pricing, volume, and other data that is typically documented). The new person may even bring a strong relationship with the seller's competitor. The seller's position of strength is suddenly at risk because he has placed too many eggs in the basket of that one personal relationship.

In some cases, sophisticated purchasing organizations create this circumstance intentionally. They rotate buyers among suppliers so that any accrued supplier goodwill can be tossed aside to make way for aggressive new demands for concessions.

Similar problems are presented when turnover occurs on the selling side. A salesperson who has successfully grown her business is promoted to a sales management role. The customer sees the replacement salesperson as fresh meat, with little of the leverage the prior salesperson had established.

In all these circumstances, an established, openly communicated CVF can mute the impact of personnel changes. While the personal relationships are important, the CVF reminds everyone that the business relationship is paramount. And a strong, documented business relationship can help the seller prosper through times of change.

A seller should develop a Customer Value File for each major customer and formally present it once or twice a year. If a company has a customer it absolutely cannot afford to lose, the CVF should be a mandatory element of the seller's relationship management.

This type of documentation is a powerful sales tool that *clearly differentiates the seller from the competition*. This differentiation can help the customer understand the risks of considering a move to another supplier.

The CVF is effective at any account, regardless of size. It is a mistake to believe that the CVF is effective at only big accounts. Although the numbers are often bigger at large accounts, in fact it is smaller companies, strapped for resources, that most appreciate the detailed report of money saved and investment received.

When considering how to use the CVF in selling, the seller should keep in mind that it is most effective when used proactively, and not in the face of crisis. More often than not, companies commit to the development of a CVF only after they see a price reduction is demanded, a loss of business is threatened, or a major mistake is made. The CVF can be helpful in these situations as well, although its value risks being discounted by the customer due to the adversarial circumstances. If, instead, the CVF is developed and presented when the waters are calm, the customer's receptivity and the chance for ultimate success are greatly enhanced.

EXAMPLES

The following case examples illustrate how companies can use the CVF to protect and reinforce important business relationships.

Case 1

A leading supplier of engineered components to the automotive industry was faced with a challenge. An aggressive new head of worldwide purchasing at its largest customer had presented a choice: Meet the customer's demand for price reductions or risk having all current parts shopped to other suppliers. The company's sales to this customer exceeded $100 million annually, so a reduction of even a few points would cost millions.

The company responded by assembling a detailed report describing the value generated for the customer and the investments made to support the customer, and subtly outlining the risks the customer would face if critical engine, steering, or transmission parts were shifted to a lesser supplier.

The leading supplier pulled together a multidisciplined team to help construct the CVF, even bringing in retired engineers who could help enumerate the many enabling innovations the company had provided to this customer during its 50-year relationship.

The end product was impressive. The report detailed millions of dollars in engineering, training, and capital equipment investments made specifically to support the customer's business. It also demonstrated more than $100 million in dollarized annual savings received by the customer due to the supplier's contributions. When multiplied over the life of the projects involved, the economic benefit totaled more than $1 billion.

The report also alerted the senior managers at the customer of the risks it could face. The supplier had shipped more than one billion parts to the customer, with a quality rate unmatched in the industry. Those parts had been delivered with 99.4 percent conformance to the customer's delivery schedules. The implication of such overwhelming facts was that any competitor the customer considered would likely perform worse, not better.

The company included other more creative elements as well. It constructed a 50-year milestone history, demonstrating how many times it helped make lightning strike in the past. The supplier also reported on a special employee incentive program that provided $1,000 in cash to any employee who purchased a new car made by the customer. This program generated nearly 700 new car sales for the customer, which represented millions of dollars in revenues and profits.

Strategically, the supplier used this presentation not just to defend against the request for price cuts, but also as a platform for discussing new engine and transmission programs. The end result was a healthy give-and-take, with the supplier earning new business commitments and the customer receiving commitments for both parties to look for new ways to save money.

Case 2

An industrial components supplier sold most of its product through large national distribution networks. Over time, those networks had become nonexclusive. That is, they carried multiple brands of most product categories. The distributor's management influenced brand selection by deciding how much of each brand to keep on the shelf at any point in time; the distributor's inside and outside salespeople had discretion over which brand to recommend on many sales.

This forced the components supplier to fight for share within its distributor. The manufacturer provided significant support to the distributor, including field engineering assistance, inventory management, promotional programs, and so on. Even though they were respected among the distributor's management team, they were concerned that they were not receiving their earned share of business despite these investments. This was exacerbated by the fact that the distributor had nearly 100 branch locations around the country. The geographic dispersion resulted in limited flow of information back to the key decision makers.

The sales team responsible for this account decided to develop a Customer Value File that could be presented periodically to the distributor's corporate management, as well as to local branch managers. The objective would be to communicate and reinforce the value provided, and to gain commitments for future initiatives that would result in incremental share gains.

Data collection would be a challenge, as several dozen of the supplier's salespeople and engineers supported the distributor's nationwide locations. The team realized that ad hoc data collection would not work, so they instead built the infrastructure required to collect and maintain the desired information on an ongoing basis.

The cornerstone of the new infrastructure was a tool built into the company's existing customer relationship management system. Each time a member of the supplier's team made a joint sales call or a technical support call, or otherwise acted to help the distributor, the team member would submit a postcall report detailing the activity and its expected impact for the distributor. After this system was up and running for several months, the supplier was able to instantly consolidate the data and to report back to the distributor in great detail.

The reports would list the number of times the supplier supported the distributor in helping an end user. The number of man-hours involved, the nature of the work, and the impact of any problems solved were also included. In addition, each call was tied to a projected impact on the distributor's sales to the end-use customer. For example, if the supplier sent a sales engineer to help solve an end user's technical problem and that resulted in the distributor earning $5,000 in annual replacement parts business, that revenue would be reported.

All of these various activities were rolled up annually and semiannually to report on the overall state of the relationship. The components supplier also included data detailing the inventory savings provided to the distributor, IT investments made to support the distributor, training provided to the distributor's staff, and other valuable elements of the relationship. The report was presented not as a defense of past work, but as a justification to consider a closer working relationship going forward.

Note: See Chapter 23 for more detail on building a CVF.

Chapter 9

Removing Doubt in the Seller's Mind

One of the great challenges for any manager is keeping employees inspired and confident in their ability to successfully accomplish their appointed tasks. Nowhere is this more difficult than with sales organizations. Unlike people in finance, production, legal, and other parts of the organization, people who sell for a living face rejection every day. Like the major league batter, who is a huge success if he prevails one out of every three attempts, the professional seller also must accept failure and rejection routinely and continue to step up to the plate each day.

One problem in protecting the confidence of salespeople is that they often work on an island. Unlike office workers who can cavort with friendly colleagues throughout the day, salespeople are out visiting customers, struggling against tough competitors, and dealing with the aftermaths of company mistakes. When faced with rejection from customers, regular price resistance, and occasional skepticism about product or service quality, it is no wonder that doubt creeps into the seller's psyche now and again.

One by-product benefit of a dollarized approach to the marketplace is that it can renew and buoy the confidence of a shaken salesperson. A seller who has begun to believe that, yes, perhaps the price is *too* high, will begin to believe in the product's true value to the customer. And the seller who has been forced to make peace after a delivery gaffe or other problem will see the mistake as a mere blip in the otherwise positive economic business relationship.

Whenever we work with a company to help them understand, articulate, and sell the value they help create, we routinely see a remarkable awakening. Salespeople and others in an organization who stand on the front line every day can become worn down by the daily skirmishes they face. Sometimes a simple exploration of the value an organization creates is enough to send the front-line team back into battle with renewed vigor.

A recent program involved a company that sells coatings to the automotive industry. Over the years, aggressive automotive buyers had demanded more and more service from the coatings company, while also exacting price reductions every step of the way. To add insult to injury, the car companies also blamed the supplier for any coating-related problem that arose. Whether or not the supplier had directly or indirectly caused the problem (it usually was not at fault), the burden was on the supplier to find the root cause and remedy the issues.

Understandably, the sales and service teams responsible for these customers were a bit downtrodden. They were stretched thin, they performed yeoman's work for their customers, and yet they were thrashed every time a contract came up for negotiation. When these teams assembled for a dollarization brainstorming session, they were initially a jaded, cynical bunch. But after a two-hour work session in which they detailed all the many elements of value they delivered for their customers, the group appeared to have emerged from a revivalist meeting. The results were astounding. Not only were there more than 100 line items of activities that were routinely provided to customers with no direct reward, but there were also countless tales of heroic feats that saved customers from peril. Each time we ran one of these drills, the sales and service teams emerged energized and proud. In some cases, they were angry at how they had allowed themselves to be taken advantage of.

Each team emerged with a renewed sense of purpose. They were proud of their contributions, and they were hungry to be recognized for those contributions. The simple act of recognizing the breadth and depth of their own contributions created a boldness and source of strength for facing down future customer demands.

REMOVING DOUBT, REMOVING EXCUSES

An aspect of dollarization that managers love and salespeople do not is that it eliminates a standard excuse for losing a sale. Selling is a tough profession, and salespeople tend to blame certain sales failures on variables beyond their control. One challenge for the manager is to eliminate these barriers to sales success so salespeople can focus on winning, rather than explaining away losses.

A classic example is paperwork. Salespeople love to complain about paperwork. They will say they are expected to do so much reporting that they have little time left to sell. But when that paperwork burden is suddenly eliminated, the salesperson typically does not become more productive.

Likewise, salespeople often blame lost sales on their company's high prices. They will explain, "If our prices were 10 percent lower, we'd have won that business." Once equipped with the tools and ability to dollarize the value of their offering, these same salespeople lose another convenient excuse. If they continue to lose close price battles despite an acknowledged value advantage, the salesperson's underperformance is exposed, just as when the burden of paperwork is vanquished.

This is not meant to be a blanket criticism of salespeople. Every day we stand shoulder to shoulder with people who sell for a living, and we appreciate the difficulty of what they do. However, salespeople who want to succeed must guard against socially acceptable reasons for failure (paperwork, prices too high) and use every weapon at their disposal to succeed.

Chapter 10

Dollarization to Get
a Prospect's Attention

Most of the discussion of dollarization in this section relates to its use when actively selling to the customer. But before that kind of selling can begin, one needs to get an appointment with the targeted decision maker. Whether you're trying to reach a new contact at an existing customer or trying to break into a new customer altogether, a dollarized approach can help you get noticed.

The decision makers you are targeting are busy, and most will guard against incoming volleys from salespeople. In order to break through, you must plan and execute an approach that will deliver a compelling, dollarized reason for the prospective customer to take notice of your offer.

Generally, a sequence similar to the following will vastly increase the odds of your gaining access to the hard-to-see customer:

1. *Send a brief one-page letter to the decision maker* before calling to set up an appointment. The letter should be crisp and to the point, and should provide an indication of the dollarized value you think you can offer the prospect (see

Figure 10.1). This estimate is based on your homework and your experience with similar companies.

2. *Always follow up your letter in a timely fashion with a phone call.* Many customers report receiving a letter and never getting any follow-up. This is a common sales failing. One reason salespeople do not follow up is because they fear rejection. They hope the customer will receive the letter, pick up the phone, and call back if interested. This is wishful thinking. The purpose of the phone call is to ask preliminary qualifying questions, further explain your dollarized story, answer the prospect's questions, and secure a face-to-face meeting.

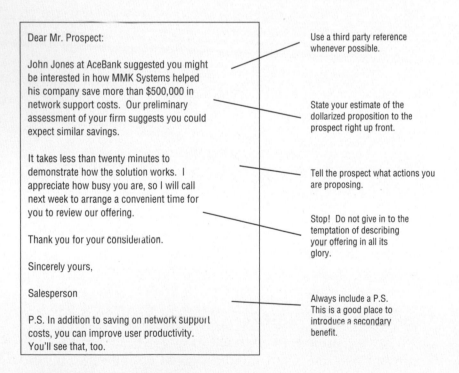

Dear Mr. Prospect:

John Jones at AceBank suggested you might be interested in how MMK Systems helped his company save more than $500,000 in network support costs. Our preliminary assessment of your firm suggests you could expect similar savings.

It takes less than twenty minutes to demonstrate how the solution works. I appreciate how busy you are, so I will call next week to arrange a convenient time for you to review our offering.

Thank you for your consideration.

Sincerely yours,

Salesperson

P.S. In addition to saving on network support costs, you can improve user productivity. You'll see that, too.

Use a third party reference whenever possible.

State your estimate of the dollarized proposition to the prospect right up front.

Tell the prospect what actions you are proposing.

Stop! Do not give in to the temptation of describing your offering in all its glory.

Always include a P.S. This is a good place to introduce a secondary benefit.

FIGURE 10.1 Sample Appointment Letter

3. *Your phone call should be prepared and practiced.* Prepare a written script, or notes, to remind yourself of exactly what you are going to say to the prospect. This should be carefully thought out, honest, and *practiced*.

Your phone call should be in the context of your letter. It should also be delivered in the same direct, businesslike, benefit-oriented style as your letter.

Sample Phone Call

Mr. Prospect, my name is Jane Salesperson, and I am following up on my letter of April 1. As I mentioned in the letter, MMK Systems helped AceBank save half a million dollars in network support costs, and we believe we can do the same for you. You will be able to judge our basic approach in less than 20 minutes. Would you allow me 15 or 20 minutes from your schedule to discuss this savings idea?

At this point, the customer may not yet agree to a meeting, but he will likely be intrigued enough to begin asking questions. The prospect of saving "half a million dollars" requires that he at least do some preliminary due diligence. To ignore such an

---

A Note on Voice Mail: Frequently, when trying to set up a call with a customer, the salesperson will reach a voice mailbox instead of a real person. This requires careful scripting of a compelling reason for the customer to respond. Do not wait until you hear the beep to begin crafting your message.

offer is management malpractice. Of course, the dollarized offer used in the letter and phone call must be realistic and credible. If the customer sees it as a smoke-and-mirrors trick to get his attention, the letter will be tossed and the phone call never taken. So be careful when crafting such messages.

Once the phone call advances to a two-way exploratory conversation between the prospect and the seller, the properly prepared salesperson should have no trouble getting the face-to-face appointment.

The Dollarized Elevator Exercise

A common sales training exercise involves salespeople condensing their sales pitch into a concise message that could be delivered at a moment's notice when unexpectedly meeting a prospective customer (for example, in an elevator).

As with the letters and phone calls described in this chapter, the effective elevator pitch should be dollarized, and the purpose of the message is simply to get the next meeting, not to make the sale on the spot. Even when precise data is not known for every prospect, the salesperson should have some credible reference for the magnitude of financial value the prospective customer might expect.

For example, the salesperson might say:

Good morning, Ms. Jones. My company specializes in finding ways to drive down the manufacturing costs of companies like yours by creatively applying our thermal engineering expertise. We can typically reduce refrigeration costs by 30 percent or more, which can amount to several hundred thousand dollars in immediate savings. Is that kind of improvement of interest to you?

GETTING ACROSS THE E-MOAT

Today's businessperson is protected from unsolicited intrusions by an ever-increasing moat of voice mail, e-mail, and ultraefficient executive assistants. This insulation makes salespeople cringe as they struggle to meet new prospects. But these barriers, though frustrating, should be looked upon as opportunities. We routinely hear salespeople complain, "If I could only get a few moments of the prospect's undivided attention, I know he would be interested in my offering." Short of a chance meeting in an elevator, voice mail is perhaps the best opportunity to deliver an uninterrupted message to your target.

Of course, the voice mail message you leave must be compelling, and it must be delivered crisply and clearly. So, just as you would sit and carefully write your letter, you must sit down and script your voice mail message before dialing the phone. You will also need to plan and practice what you will say in the rare event the prospect answers your call personally.

TRYING THE UNORTHODOX

Occasionally, difficult prospecting territory will warrant bringing in the heavy artillery. Particularly in situations where the number of prospects is limited and the potential business value of each is substantial, it makes sense to put additional resources into the prospecting effort. Creativity will help, too. Consider this example.

Great Northern Energy,* a large Midwestern electric utility, had developed a unique competence in its management of

---

*The name Great Northern Energy has been substituted to protect the confidentiality of the company discussed in this case study.

collections—the capture of past-due and delinquent customer charges. The team had become so efficient that Great Northern created a business unit that would sell various collection services to other utilities. Initial efforts faced tough resistance, in large part due to a flaw in the unit's strategic plan: attempting to sell "outsourced collections services" to collections managers at utilities. Since these collections managers' power bases at their utilities were directly correlated to the number of employees they had under their supervision, an outsourcing strategy was, in effect, a direct threat to their authority.

After struggling with this barrier for several months, Great Northern changed direction. It conducted an analysis of the benefits delivered to customers and developed a dollarization story that demonstrated significant financial impacts to large utilities. Great Northern's initial pro forma analyses showed it could improve the earnings of a typical large utility by the equivalent of several cents per share. Armed with this knowledge, Great Northern set its sights on the utility CFOs.

Realizing that it enjoyed zero awareness among the targeted CFOs, Great Northern launched a marketing and publicity blitz to establish credibility. It also developed a unique program for breaking through to key prospects.

Great Northern analyzed the public financial data for the nation's largest utilities and narrowed the target list to those that appeared to have higher than average receivables problems. Then, also based on the public data, Great Northern would complete a thorough pro forma dollarization analysis for the target utility.

Recognizing the challenge of breaking through to utility CFOs, Great Northern developed a novel strategy for securing appointments. For each prospective customer, the Great Northern unit's president would make a personalized recording of a carefully scripted, two-minute message to the target CFO (see Figure 10.2).

Hello, John. My name is Tom Smith. I'm president of Great Northern A/R Services, one of the unregulated companies of Great Northern Energy. For 20 years, Great Northern A/R Services has been providing cash flow improvement solutions exclusively to utilities. The focus is reducing write-offs, speeding up cash flow, and reducing days receivables outstanding.

Great Northern stresses early intervention in the receivables process to improve utilities' financial health. Great Northern actually reduces the number of delinquent accounts and subsequent write-offs. Based on our preliminary analysis of your company's revenues and write-offs, Great Northern believes it can increase your annual net income by several million dollars. How? By implementing three cash flow improvement tools that require no capital investment on your part. Early Contact, key to the Great Northern cash improvement strategy, will generate cash for you immediately. It involves telephoning delinquent active accounts to stop problems before they get out of hand. Early Contact dovetails with your customer service operations, giving you predictive dialing results without the capital investment, training, staffing, or overhead problems. The next tool is called Skip Alert. It's an interutility database that not only locates debtors, but also identifies high-risk utility users at turn-on, enabling you to get deposit protection. Finally, Capture is an automated miscellaneous billing system, giving you timely and comprehensive invoicing of all nonenergy charges. Capture also works with your existing delinquent bill follow-up procedures.

Citizens' write-offs are now costing you $41,000 a day, and every five-hundredths of 1 percent improvement in your write-off rate means one and a half million dollars more net annual income. We should set up a Great Northern A/R Services cash flow review as soon as possible to document specific savings for you. I'll call you in the next few days. Thank you for your time.

FIGURE 10.2 Sample Great Northern Audio Script

This message would be recorded on a cassette tape, which would be loaded into a compact, battery-operated tape player. Great Northern's marketing staff would call each target CFO's office to inquire when the prospect would next be in his or her office. The tape player would be delivered via Federal Express overnight service so it was waiting on the CFO's desk upon arrival. The package also contained a note asking the CFO to hit "play" for a brief personalized message. The program enabled Great Northern to gain appointments with more than 60 percent of their targets, and firmly positioned the firm as a high-level cash flow consultant (not as a boiler-room collections agency).

Chapter 11

Dollarization and Channel Partners

Many businesses depend on "channel partners" to handle the direct selling function with the ultimate end customer. These intermediaries may be dealers, distributors, brokers, value-added resellers, agents, or take any of a number of other forms.

The effective marketer (or "principal") understands that his or her offering must create value for the ultimate end user of the product or service. Without this creation of value, neither the principal nor the channel partner has anything to sell. But what many principals overlook is that they must also create value for their channel partners.

Channel partners, whatever form they take, are in business to serve their owners and customers, not their principals. Typically, the channel partner represents several principals, and must make choices as to how to allocate resources and attention among those principals. The challenge for the principal is to persuade the channel partner to invest more resources on the principal's behalf. Dollarization is an effective tool for encouraging that kind of shift.

Too often, we see principals trying heavy-handed means to direct the channel partner. They take the channel partner for granted and create an adversarial relationship rather than one that is truly symbiotic. By shifting the conversation to dollarized value in the channel partner's pocket, the principal lets the channel partner understand that the thinking has changed. The principal who dollarizes recognizes that his success depends on the success he helps create for his partner.

CASE HISTORIES

The following case histories illustrate how companies have used dollarization to motivate their channel partners.

Example 1

The Cameron Group* is a leading provider of retirement plans to small and medium-sized businesses. Cameron relies on a network of independent financial consultants (aka stockbrokers) as its channel to the market. Cameron's perennial challenge is to get these independent financial consultants to focus on an activity with which they are largely unfamiliar.

The Cameron Group recognized that all financial consultants share one attribute: They want to make money! Recognizing this, the Cameron sales and marketing team developed a selling strategy based on the dollarized value to the financial consultant of selling Cameron retirement plans.

Cameron first collected and studied available company data and industry research to make a dollarized case for why a

---

*The name Cameron Group has been substituted to protect the confidentiality of the company discussed in this case study.

broker should invest selling time to help Cameron sell retirement plans.

The story they compiled was compelling: For every two customers a broker introduced to a Cameron retirement plan specialist, one would become a retirement plan customer (that is, Cameron had a 50 percent historical hit rate). As shown in Table 11.1, the average retirement plan produced $7,000 in income for the broker over the first year, and studies demonstrated that, on average, every dollar of retirement plan income represented $3 in potential incremental sales to the broker. This translated to a three-year total of $63,000 in incremental income for the broker, just for introducing two clients to Cameron. With a historical hit rate of 50 percent, each introductory sales call represented a three-year value of $31,500 (50% × $63,000) or a first-year expected value of $10,500.

The Cameron specialists crafted and practiced the following pitch:

> If you and I can get in front of a qualified retirement plan opportunity, we have a 50 percent chance, based on my numbers last year and industry averages, of adding $21,000 a year to your gross commission for three years or more. Does that type of number interest you?

TABLE 11.1 Value of a Cameron Sales Call

Retirement Plan Value	$7,000
× Multiplier Effect on New Business	3
= Total Annual Value to Broker	$21,000
× Historical Hit Rate	50%
= Expected Value of Sales Call	$10,500
× Expected Life of New Business Impact (Years)	3
= Total Expected Value of Cameron Sales Call	$31,500

Example 2

The Barchester Company* relied on industrial distributors to serve the fractured industrial maintenance and repair market. The independent distributors that carried Barchester's product also carried several other brands of the same product. When a customer called asking for a 3-inch bearing, the distributor could select from several options. It was therefore critical for Barchester to persuade its distributors that their interests were best served when Barchester products were specified.

For many years, Barchester accomplished this in the field, where its corps of sales engineers traveled with distributor salespeople and helped them solve technical problems for customers. This helped Barchester with the local branch sales reps, who directly benefited from the expert assistance. But gradually, more and more decision making was shifting to distributor headquarters. For example, even if a local distributor rep preferred to sell a Barchester product, he was often forced to sell a competitor's product because headquarters had decided to stock the shelves with another brand.

Ultimately, Barchester realized it needed to tell its story at the highest levels of its distribution partners. It developed a data-collection system so that all the detailed activity that happened at dozens of distributor branch locations could be consolidated in one report. Barchester assembled a detailed economic sum-

---

*The name Barchester Company has been substituted to protect the confidentiality of the company discussed in this case study.

mary that illustrated all the investments made to support the distributor's business, and also calculated the return the distributor earned from selling Barchester products.

This information was presented periodically to the distributor's management. Barchester used these presentations to demonstrate the financial advantage to the distributor of carrying the Barchester line. The value presentations helped Barchester to protect its existing share at the distributor and to get commitments for additional stocking and marketing by the distributor.

Example 3

Another industrial products company sold heavily through distribution and operated under the motto, "A distributor will make us money, but first we must make them money." The entire sales and marketing organization was trained to focus on innovative ways to help improve a distributor's revenues and reduce a distributor's costs. Each year as part of the business planning process, the team responsible for selling through a major distributor would tally the economic value delivered to the distributor. The worksheet shown in Figure 11.1 was used to document the economic activity that occurred on the distributor's behalf.

1. **JIT Delivery: Reduced Carrying Costs**
    - Reduction in Inventory   _____
    - × Annual Inventory Carrying Cost   _____
    - **= Carrying Cost Savings**   _____

2. **Reduced Transaction Cost Savings**
    - Reduction in Number of Transactions Processed   _____
    - × Cost per Transaction   _____
    - **= Transaction Cost Savings**   _____

3. **On-Time Delivery**
    - Reduction in Distributor Inventory Due to
      On-Time Delivery   _____
    - × Annual Inventory Carrying Cost   _____
    - **= Value of On-time Delivery**   _____

4. **Value of Direct Accounts Turned Over to Distributor**
    - Annual Sales to Account   _____
    - × Average Gross Margin   _____
    - **= Annual Value to Distributor**   _____

5. **Drag-Along Sales**
    - Drag-Along Sales   _____
    - × Average Gross Margin   _____
    - **= Annual Value to Distributor**   _____

6. **Value of Electronic Data Interface**
    - Reduced Order Placement Costs   _____
    - + Value of Automatic Identification of
      Competitor Part Numbers   _____
    - **= Order Placement Savings**   _____
    - Reduction in Distributor Inventory Due
      to EDI Efficiency   _____
    - × Annual Inventory Carrying Cost   _____
    - = Value of On-Time Delivery   _____
    - **= Total EDI Value**   _____

FIGURE 11.1 Distributor Cost Savings and Investment Returns Worksheet

INVESTMENTS TO SUPPORT DISTRIBUTOR
1. **Distributor Training Seminars**
   - Number of People Attending _____
   - × Number of Days Training _____
   - = Training Man-days _____
   - × Value per Training Man-day _____
   - **= Distributor Training Investment** _____
2. **Distributor Plant Maintenance Seminars**
   - Number of People Attending _____
   - × Number of Days Training _____
   - = Training Man-days _____
   - × Value per Training Man-day _____
   - **= Distributor Training Investment** _____
   - + Resultant Drag-Along Sales _____
   - **= Total Value of Plant Maintenance Seminars** _____
3. **Engineering Services**
   - Number of Engineering Man-days _____
   - × Value of Engineering Man-day _____
   - **= Engineering Investment** _____
   - + Value of Engineering Recommendations/
     Solutions _____
   - + Resultant Drag-Along Sales _____
   - **= Total Value of Engineering Services** _____
4. **Value of Free Samples**
   - Market Value of Free Samples _____
5. **Marketing Investments**
   - End-User Advertising Investment _____
   - + Value of Free Trade Show Displays _____
   - + Value of Sales/Promotional Literature _____
   - + Value of Joint Mailing Participation _____
   - + Value of Catalog Inserts _____
   - **= Total Marketing Investments** _____
GRAND TOTAL _____

FIGURE 11.1 *(Continued)*

Chapter 12

Dollarizing and Selling Services

Every week, it seems, we get calls, letters, and e-mails from companies observing that our past writings on dollarization use tangible products as examples. Rarely do we talk, we're told, about how dollarization applies to *services*. Many of these same observers also conclude, based largely on our lack of attention, that dollarization in fact cannot be applied to a service business, or at the very least it is much more difficult to do so.

None of this is true. Our tendency to use tangible products in examples (of which we are guilty in this book as well) is based more on habit and for the sake of clear examples than anything else. And while service businesses do present certain unique challenges, there is no inherent reason why one could not dollarize a service as one would a product.

Marketers and sellers of any offering—product and service alike—must always remember that customers do not buy products *or* services. Instead, they buy the benefits that result from these products and services. And when a business buys a product or service, they are ultimately buying the dollarized value of those benefits.

For example, if a company needs to get a document across town, both a human courier (a service) and a fax machine (a product) could get the job done. Similarly, a company that needs to shred its documents for security purposes can buy a paper shredder (a product) or outsource the activity to a mobile document shredding service. In both examples, the company is buying an outcome, which might be achieved by multiple means. It is these *outcomes* that can be dollarized.

So the distinction of product versus service is not always a relevant factor. What is a more relevant factor is the presence (or lack) of meaningful points of difference. Just as it is difficult to dollarize one product over other nearly identical offerings, it is also difficult to dollarize the value of one service offering over other largely indistinguishable service offerings. It *is* true that distinguishing similar service offerings can be more challenging than distinguishing similar product offerings. Let's look at why this is so.

For example, two widgets may differ by just .0001 inches, but that difference, though small, is measurable, repeatable, and provable to a customer. Meanwhile, two accomplished lawyers may have similar but slightly different capabilities, but demonstrating that difference to a prospective client may prove practically impossible (or impractical). To better understand this, it is helpful to review the fundamental differences between products and services (see Figure 12.1).

Interestingly, some service companies have found that dollarization can be used to reverse the effect described in Figure 12.1. Rather than allow the intangible nature of their service offerings to preclude them from attempting dollarization, these companies instead *use dollarization as a strategy to make their services tangible.*

Intangible	Perishable
A service can't be touched before purchase.	A service can't be stored for later use.
Inseparable	**Variable**
A service can't be separated from its provider.	The quality of a service depends on who provides the service.

FIGURE 12.1 Characteristics That Make Services Different from Products

For example, ColorTec Automotive Coatings* developed a service business to provide outsourced services to its automotive clients. For each key service offered, the ColorTec team developed a detailed cost calculator (see Figure 12.2), which specified all the activities covered by the service, as well as any related cost areas that could be impacted. When ColorTec worked through this economic model with a customer, the visible, tangible cost calculator became a proxy for the service offering under consideration. This approach enabled the ColorTec service business to grow from nothing to more than $60 million in annual sales in a few short years.

Similarly, Engel Document Services† launched a business in

---

*The name ColorTec Automotive Coatings has been substituted to protect the confidentiality of the company discussed in this case study.

†The name Engel Document Services has been substituted to protect the confidentiality of the company discussed in this case study.

			Facility Name:	Acme Auto
Enter Data for Your Facility			Proposal Date:	May 1, 2004

Paint Line Cleaning - Operating Cost Comparison

	Key Parameters	As Planned
Enter:	# Cleanings Per Year	5
Enter:	# Vehicles Produced Per Year	250,000
Enter:	Fully Loaded Cost Per Hour (mra)	$ 54.00
Enter:	Fully Loaded Cost Per Hour (sko)	$ 57.00
Enter:	Fully Loaded Cost Per Hour (sal)	$ 60.00
Enter:	Fully Loaded Cost Per Hour (supv)	$ 67.50

	Material Cost - Paint Line Cleaning	As Planned
Enter:	Resin Cost Per Cleaning	$ –
Enter:	Purge Cost Per Cleaning	$ –
Enter:	Stripper Cost Per Cleaning	$ –

	Manpower Cost - Paint Line Cleaning	As Planned
Enter:	# Associates (mra)	4.00
Enter:	# Hours Per Person Per Cleaning (mra)	33.00
Enter:	# Associates (sko)	2.00
Enter:	# Hours Per Person Per Cleaning (sko)	8.00
Enter:	# Associates (sal)	1.00
Enter:	# Hours Per Person Per Cleaning (sal)	4.00
Enter:	# Associates (supv)	1.00
Enter:	# Hours Per Person Per Cleaning (supv)	2.00

FIGURE 12.2 ColorTec Economic Value Analysis

the early 1990s focused on outsourcing mail-room services at large corporations. Engel's marketing strategy was innovative, successfully positioning the mail-room decision as a meaningful financial issue for a client CFO/CEO (versus a staffing decision by the mail-room manager, whose self-importance was often gauged by the number of employees on his staff). Engel used a cost evaluation tool that enabled the customer to project potential cost savings, again making real what otherwise would be intangible.

A software services firm used this approach to introduce its offering to Fortune 500 companies. The approach worked so well that after one initial dollarization review, the prospective customer was more interested in buying the diagnostic calculator than in the seller's software solutions.

Another way to make intangible services tangible is to document case history successes and to use those cases when selling to future customers. These cases can serve multiple purposes. They can help illustrate how a service helped past customers, including the dollarized value of those past results. They can help make a complex or unfamiliar service offering "real" by illustrating it with real-life examples. And they can help a customer internalize how a service might apply to his or her business situation. Case histories can also be developed to highlight specific capabilities. A manufacturing consulting firm used a case history approach as a key strategy in communicating its capabilities to prospective customers (see Figure 12.3).

Sellers of services can also benefit from a dollarization focus in other ways. First, a focus on potential dollarized value can help to differentiate one company from others selling similar services. For example, a chief information officer (CIO) who is bombarded by pitches from dozens of IT services firms may find those offers indistinguishable, as they all ramble on about outsourced services, better asset utilization, improved data accessibility, and so on. But if one company were to instead propose an opportunity "to save $300,000, to reduce call center wait times by 40 percent, and to eliminate $4.2 million in assets by consolidating network services," there is a very good chance those offers would rise to the top of the CIO's pile (as they did for a leading provider of IT solutions). Even without a tight estimate of the dollarized value, a customer will know you are focused on the customer's problem, not on your offer, which in itself will differentiate you from competition.

Ringleader
Precision Steel Solutions

application case history

Customer Reduces Scrap by 75%.
Saves $1 Million on Gear Application.

Prior Situation:
Customer was scrapping 26% of its finished internal planetary gears due to out-of-round and distortion problems.

The Ringleader PSS Solution:
Ringleader assessed the customer's materials and processes and identified the customer's steel specification as the main contributor to the high scrap rate. Specifically, when broached, the steel would incur stresses that led to distortion during heat treat. With Ringleader materials science expertise, a better alloy steel grade was recommended. The grade showed improved microstructure, lower hardness and higher sulfur content which delivered the machinability characteristics required for this application.

Specific Benefits to Customer:

- Better machinability of the gear steel resulted in a reduction of undesirable machining stresses and reduced distortion during heat treat. This cut the customer's scrap rate from 26% to less than 6%, saving more than $1 million per year.

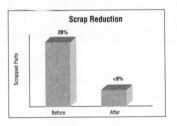

- Better machinability of the steel also resulted in 50% longer tool life for the customer's broaching tools. Each broaching tool costs approximately $50,000.

- In addition, the improved machinability also eliminated the need for manual inspection and chip removal, which enabled the customer to redeploy an employee away from this low value-added task.

- The reduction in distortion enabled the customer to better contol and hold the geometry of the finished gears. This improved gear mesh and reduced gear noise in operation.

FIGURE 12.3 Case History Approach
Note: The name Ringleader has been substituted to protect the confidentiality of the company discussed in this case study.

Before Dollarizing	After
New business pitches focus on education, experience, and processes used in delivery of service.	New business pitches focus on client problems and the value to the client of solving these problems.

FIGURE 12.4 Before and After Dollarizing

In addition, a dollarization focus can have indirect benefits on a service company's sales productivity. We have found that service providers—especially professional service providers, where the same person who sells the service provides the service (attorneys, consultants, etc.)—become much more customer focused after being exposed to the concept of dollarization. The transformation works as shown in Figure 12.4.

DOLLARIZATION AND MARKETING

Quality in a product or service is not what the supplier puts in. It is what the customer gets out and is willing to pay for. A product is not quality because it is hard to make and costs a lot of money, as manufacturers typically believe. This is incompetence. Customers pay only for what is of use to them and gives them value. Nothing else constitutes quality.

—Peter Drucker

What we obtain too cheap, we esteem too lightly;'tis dearness only that gives everything its value.

—Thomas Paine

Chapter 13

Dollarization and Marketing Communications

The writings of the great advertising man David Ogilvy are full of valuable tips and insights that could sharpen any marketing communications program. One of his themes in particular, the intentional use of facts and numbers in marketing language, is critical in business-to-business marketing. Dollarization is a sure route to making those numbers even more hard-hitting.

Ogilvy on Advertising

Avoid superlatives, generalizations, and platitudes. Be specific and factual.[1]

Every word in the copy must count. Concrete figures must be substituted for atmospheric claims; clichés must give way to facts, and empty exhortations to alluring offers.[2]

For businesses, what could be a more "alluring offer" than cold, hard cash?

Volumes and volumes have been written on advertising development, positioning, and related topics. We don't intend to retrace every step in the process. (The discussion of "advertising"

123

in this chapter is intended to apply to all traditional marketing communications, including ads, print collateral, direct mail, and online support. We have selected print advertising as a medium for illustrating our observations because it provides a concise encapsulation of the key concepts.)

In our experience, much business-to-business advertising is an afterthought. Rarely do we see communications that effectively differentiate the marketer from competition, and rarely do we see a compelling reason to buy. Upon meeting a prospective new client, one of our first steps is to review the available literature, marketing plans, and website. Nine times out of 10, we find soft descriptions. Adjectives and modifiers such as "more," "faster," and "better" are employed to do the work that numbers could perform so much more effectively. We ask clients to try to put themselves in their prospective customers' shoes. What does the prospect learn from reading such adjectives? The prospect learns nothing that will enable him to make a decision.

Good advertising is predicated on solid positioning, which of course requires a clear understanding of the target segment's needs, attitudes, and so on. Positioning also requires a clear understanding of how the marketer's offering will fulfill the unique needs and wishes of the segment. The traditional path to message development is shown in Figure 13.1.

We find adding an additional step to this process creates a crisper, more effective message (see Figure 13.2).

[Segmentation → Positioning → Unique Selling Proposition (USP)]

FIGURE 13.1 Traditional Message Development Path

[Segmentation → Positioning → **Dollarized Selling Proposition (DSP)**]

FIGURE 13.2 Message Development Path with Dollarization

The dollarized selling proposition (DSP) is like the traditional USP in that it boils down the unique essence of why the customer should be interested in the offering. However, unlike the USP, the DSP states the proposition in terms of the financial gain that a customer can expect. By creating a sharp DSP, the business-to-business marketer will find the creative acts of advertising concept development, headline development, and copywriting much easier. The entire creative effort focuses on the customer's bottom line, not the product's pretty package.

THE GOOD, THE BAD, AND THE UGLY

A review of business-to-business advertising reveals a full spectrum of quality: the ugly, the bad, and the good. Occasionally, it will also include some very good, even great executions.

Ugly

These ads use puns and borrowed interest in an effort to cleverly get the customer's attention. To borrow again from David Ogilvy: "Some copywriters write *tricky headlines*—puns, literary allusions, and other obscurities. This is a sin."[3]

In a single edition of a recent pharmaceutical industry magazine, the following headlines and visuals appeared:

- "Bet the Pharm."
- "Definitive Performance" (which tells the reader nothing, and is further confused by a glossy photograph of a yellow Ferrari).
- "The Whole Enchilada" (with a photo of an actual enchilada. The ad, by the way, is for a vacuum pump manufacturer.).

Bad

These ads typically talk about the company and/or the product or service, but do not communicate benefits to the customer. Often, the headlines on these ads can be interchanged without altering the meaning or impact of the advertisement.

Examples:

- "A Higher Level."
- "The New Standard."
- "Experience the Difference."

Good

Good ads talk about customer benefits and they give the customer a reason to find the offering interesting, but they lack a truly compelling hook. These ads can be effective when a customer is actively searching for a solution and happens to find it buried in an ad.

Great

Great ads immediately let the target customer know that there is an option to improve the customer's business situation. The great ad is compelling and provides new information that helps the customer's business. A great ad does not necessarily need to be DSP-driven, but the presence of a clear DSP certainly improves the odds.

VALUE IN ADVERTISING

One category of advertising that is always of interest to us is the ad that uses the word "value" or "value-added" or some such derivative in the headline or copy. This tells us that the marketer is getting very close to the essence of the story. However, the evolution of the message is incomplete, either because the marketer has failed to discover and dollarize the real value or because the marketer has not discovered the right creative vehicle for articulating the story.

While the application of dollarization in advertising and marketing communications can take many forms, it is typically best executed using the following devices:

- *Testimonials:* A customer or other expert provides a third-party reporting of the dollarized story.
- *Case histories:* The marketer relates the experience of prior customers in describing the dollarized outcomes.
- *Head-to-head comparisons:* The marketer states the dollarized advantages of its product versus a prominent competitive offering.
- *Test-driven data:* The marketer reports test data (third-party or its own) that demonstrates a dollarized advantage for its product versus the competition.

The advertisements shown in Figure 13.3 are solid examples of dollarization-driven advertising.

FIGURE 13.3   Dollarization-Driven Advertising

FIGURE 13.3 *(Continued)*

How $15 saves you hundreds. Introducing the Siemon Pico Protector.™

New high-speed secondary line protection that saves valuable communications systems.

$15⁰⁰

$600⁻

Don't risk losing voice and data communications.

Electrical storms, mishandled AC power lines, static discharge and common voltage fluctuations can ruin expensive communications equipment and your business operations. For $15 per line, Pico Protector eliminates the risk.

Pico Protector responds in a pico-second; one million times faster than ordinary protection. Solid state technology stops repeated electrical spikes, and voltage surges that get past

Install Pico Protector in seconds on industry standard 66 blocks.

slower gas-tube or carbon devices. Replaceable fuses prevent equipment damage and fire hazard caused by sneak current. ⓊL Listed Signal Circuit Protector.

Call toll-free 1-800-237-1371.

For complete technical information, and the name of your Siemon Company distributor, call The Siemon Company today.

THE
SIEMON COMPANY

P.O. Box 400, 76 Westbury Park Road
Watertown, Connecticut 06795, (203) 274-2523
Pico Protector is a trademark of The Siemon Company

FIGURE 13.3   *(Continued)*

"I was having nightmares over downtime, until I accepted the Applied Challenge.

Now, I'm sleeping sweet- with $192,000 in savings."

"We'd been having problems with the conveyor drive on several of our machines, so we called Applied to help us out. They immediately recommended a different unit which would give us a lot longer life. But Applied didn't stop there. They had the replacement parts specially flown in; they picked them up at the airport and personally delivered them; and then they even helped install them! All in all, Applied's strategy and hustle saved us over $190,000 – and that's huge!"

Our DVA℠ (Documented Value-Added) Program ceaselessly searches for ways to save our customers money, whether by increasing their uptime, reducing their maintenance costs, sharpening their inventory management, cutting their energy costs or redesigning their system.

The Applied Challenge.
We challenge you to let us help you run your business more successfully, while our powerful DVA Program documents the savings every step of the way. What have you got to lose?

Then we <u>document</u> these savings for you through a customized software program that enables a consistent reporting of savings across your entire company.

For a personal explanation of our DVA Program, contact our branch nearest you or write us at Applied Industrial Technologies, One Applied Plaza, Cleveland, OH 44115-5019. Visit the Customer Jubilation section of our Web site at www.appliedindustrial.com

This Production Manager of a regional beverage manufacturer measures his day, not in hours, but in dollars per minute.

△ APPLIED
Industrial Technologies
Circle 205

This is a dramatization of a true customer case history and is fully documented in our files.

FIGURE 13.3   *(Continued)*

FIGURE 13.3 *(Continued)*

FIGURE 13.3   *(Continued)*

DOLLARIZATION AND ADVERTISING CASE EXAMPLES

The following cases illustrate how dollarization can lead to clear positioning, messaging, and communication.

Case 1

Sandvik Coromant is the world's leading maker of highly engineered carbide metal cutting tools. These tools are used heavily in the automotive and aerospace industries, and in nearly every industrial segment for shaping steel and other metals, drilling holes, threading bolts, and many other applications.

Sandvik is a prolific new product marketer. Every year, it introduces thousands of new products. These products are built on technological improvements—sometimes incremental, sometimes revolutionary. The improvements tend to focus on a few key performance areas:

- Extending tool life (more cuts per tool).
- Faster cutting (more cuts per hour).
- Improving quality of cutting (smoother surfaces, tighter tolerances).

An implicit side effect of these improvements is that the consumption of tools by customers can decrease over time. For example, if a tool that currently cuts 100 pieces before breaking is replaced by a new tool that lasts for 200 cuts, the number of tools required by that customer is theoretically cut in half. Over time, this creates a governor for unit growth, so

Sandvik must try to price its products to reflect the performance improvements to the customer in order to avoid long-term revenue erosion.

Every new product that Sandvik launches is backed by detailed comparative test data, developed by the product marketing teams. This data illustrates performance claims that can later be tested at individual customers. Every Sandvik salesperson is equipped with analytical tools to estimate the financial payback on converting to new Sandvik tooling. Dollarized thinking pervades the entire Sandvik approach to marketing, including its print advertising, which has distinguished itself from industry competitors for years (see Figure 13.4).

Case 2

Several years ago, specialty-chemical maker GAF Chemicals (subsequently renamed ISP) was facing a strategic challenge. The imminent expiration of a patent on GAF's successful and versatile solvent molecule (called M-Pyrol) threatened the potential demise of a profitable business line. The company anticipated that large, low-cost chemical companies would begin manufacturing M-Pyrol, and GAF would struggle to remain competitive as market prices plummeted.

In anticipation of these developments, GAF formulated a brilliant strategy. Using the M-Pyrol molecule as its base, GAF created a series of branded cleaners and degreasers, each targeted at a specific market and application niche.

The strategy was as simple as it was clever. By creating several small, defensible niche markets (instead of one large generic market), GAF would be able to stay below the radar screens of the large chemical makers. The niches would be too

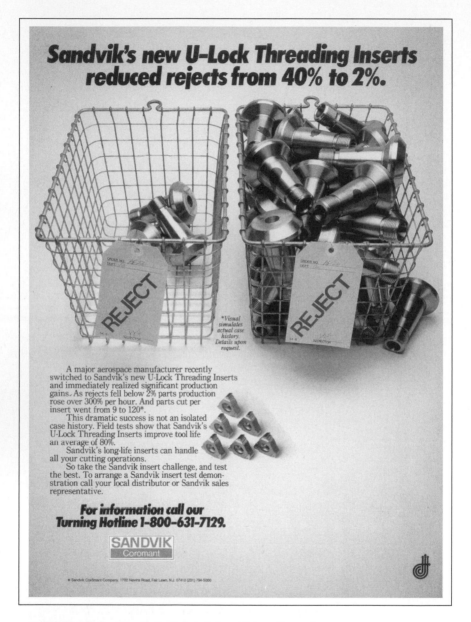

FIGURE 13.4   Sandvik Print Advertising Samples

Coromant Delta Drill:™

HSS methods:

15 mins. 120 holes.

15 mins. 17 holes.

Eliminate any or all centering, boring and reaming operations with the short-hole, cost cutting Coromant Delta Drill. It penetrates 3 to 4 times faster than conventional drills *and* produces hole tolerances of ± .0015" with 40-80 Ra surface finishes.

Self-centering TiN-coated, carbide-tipped cutting edge with revolutionary new geometry.

Use it in drill units, engine, turret, automatic and NC lathes and machining centers to dramatically lower cost-per-hole. Also improve chip control in difficult material and get better machine efficiency by increasing cutting data.

The Coromant Delta Drill effectively drills depths up to 3½ times its diameter and is available in 40 stocked standard sizes in 0.010" increments from 0.39 to 0.79"

20% off on Coromant Delta Drills for a limited time. Call our Drilling Hotline 1-800-631-7129.

DRILLING GUIDE

Free Drilling Guide helps you save even more!

SANDVIK
Coromant

● Sandvik Coromant Company, 1702 Nevins Road, Fair Lawn, N.J. 07410 (201) 794-5000

FIGURE 13.4 *(Continued)*

small for the big guys to take notice, but when combined, would represent a substantial opportunity for GAF.

To execute this strategy, GAF immersed itself in each niche. The company priced the branded products according to the value to each market, and it created packaging, literature, and advertising that directly supported the dollarized selling proposition of each product.

A good example is ShipShape Resin Cleaner, GAF's product for cleaning cured fiberglass in the boatbuilding industry, among others. The main competition for ShipShape was acetone, a cheap solvent that evaporated quickly and produced emissions laden with volatile organic compounds (VOCs). The technically oriented team at first focused on this evaporation issue from an environmental safety perspective. However, they soon learned that customers would not pay much of a premium for an environmental benefit unless they were pressed to do so by regulation or looming penalties. A second pass discovered a more direct route. Acetone's fast evaporation meant that customers were buying much more acetone than they were actually using. By comparing the evaporation rates between acetone and ShipShape, GAF discovered that customers would need to buy 17 gallons of acetone for every gallon of ShipShape. Suddenly, ShipShape's pricing premium wasn't so daunting (see Figure 13.5).

GAF proceeded to develop a launch plan that leaned on that 17× difference in evaporation and the purchase differential it would create. The company equipped salespeople to help customers justify the switch within their companies, and even ran a "Buried Treasure" activity at trade shows to engage customers in the quest for savings.

FIGURE 13.5 Dollarization-Inspired ShipShape Advertisement

Case 3

A start-up company with a novel design for a high-capacity toner cartridge for laser printers faced a tricky marketing challenge. The company, then named RTI, Inc., faced two groups of foes: the premium-priced, premium-quality industry giants and the low-priced, marginal-quality remanufacturers (thousands of shops that refilled and recycled used cartridges).

The challenge was to earn pricing in the league of the major players and not be sullied as another low-quality remanufacturer. Dollarization helped show RTI the way.

The company leaned on its unique, patented advantage—more printed pages per cartridge—to create its own niche. RTI conducted testing with third-party laboratories that consistently showed that their product produced at least twice as many printed pages as the corresponding cartridges from the market leaders. RTI also had independent imaging experts analyze the quality of the printed images to verify that RTI produced images at least as good as the big players (this was an area where remanufacturers performed poorly).

To determine possible product pricing levels, RTI used a detailed dollarization analysis to develop a cost-per-page comparison for its cartridge versus leading competitors. The analysis showed that the cartridge saved a half to a full cent per printed page in toner costs. RTI then looked at the other major consumable in laser printing: paper. It turns out that common copier paper often sells for a half to a full cent per page. In other words, the toner cartridge savings paid for the paper on which each page was printed.

The results of this analysis became one of the cornerstones of the company's branding and communications platform. First, RTI renamed the company "Clarity Imaging Technology" and the product was rebranded "PageMax." The name "Clarity" helped deflect potential marketplace concerns about the image quality produced by the company's cartridges, while "PageMax" reinforced the product's direct performance advantage.

Second, Clarity used the insight gained from its dollarization analysis to create a communications plan that instantly rendered the financial impact of its product. All advertising and marketing materials carried the tagline:

PageMax. It's like getting your paper for free.

The company supported this marketing execution by equipping salespeople with analytical tools for helping customers assess their own potential savings from switching to PageMax. The initial marketing launch plan even included plans for a promotional offer that would give customers a coupon for free paper when they bought their first PageMax cartridge.

Chapter 14

Pricing New Products

Pricing a new product is a daunting challenge for the business-to-business marketer. Price it too high, and you could face a warehouse full of unsold goods. Price it too low, and you may never recapture its true earning potential.

The new product marketer must consider many variables when determining the pricing window: segmentation, competition, market demand, differentiation, product performance, sales cycle. In our experience, few marketers also consider the dollarized value of their new products when setting the price. As a result, "80 to 90 percent of all poorly chosen prices are too low."[1]

One problem is that many new products are rushed to market, without sufficient time or commitment to gain an accurate understanding of the product's true performance advantages and the value created by those advantages. This rush is partially driven by a company's desire to see its years of investment and perseverance begin to generate payback.

Another contributing factor is the frequent pileup caused by delays in design, development, testing, and manufacturing start-up. These delays conspire to compress the launch schedule to the point where inadequate time remains for diligent marketing preparation. (Ideally, much of the marketing work—including pricing—is done early in the development cycle, but real-world observation tells us this is the exception rather than the rule.)

In other cases, companies are simply myopic or just plain timid. The most common error we see is the setting of prices based on a target gross margin, or target markup, based on the cost of the product. This is a cost-recovery pricing strategy, and has nothing to do with the marketplace. Yes, cost-driven margin analysis is a critical step in identifying pricing floors (below which prices are not commercially viable). However, the cost of making a product is irrelevant to the customer. Because target margin pricing does not consider the value of the product in use to potential customers, it has very little application in evaluating market pricing options.

Other companies take an incremental approach. They base their new product pricing decisions on a limited, direct comparison to existing, available products. If they have been selling widgets for $2, they might think their new, improved product is worth 10 percent more, or $2.20. This is without thinking through the economic implications of the advantages the new product offers.

To illustrate, McKinsey consultants Michael Marn, Eric Roegner, and Craig Zawada recently observed that, fearing the risks of slow penetration, companies "take an incremental approach to pricing: They use existing products as their reference point. If a new offering costs 15 percent more to build than the older version does, for instance, they charge about 15 percent more for it."[2]

In the same article, Marn, Roegner, and Zawada further observe:

> Good pricing decisions are based on an expansive rather than an incremental approach. Before zeroing in on a price

that promises the greatest long-term profitability, companies must know both the highest and lowest prices they could charge.[3]

Acknowledging that new product pricing is an inherently imperfect combination of marketing art and science, there are ways to add more science to the mix. New product pricing should not be strictly formulaic, as in target margin pricing, nor should it be a game of blindman's buff. Understanding the dollarized value of an offering to the target customer group is a critical ingredient to seeing new product pricing options more clearly.

DOLLARIZING YOUR WAY TO NEW PRODUCT PRICING

The following sequence can be adapted for different product types and different markets, but the essential discipline remains the same:

1. Estimate the product's dollarized value.
2. Compare the dollarized value to the price floor.
3. Consider the target customer's investment criteria.
4. Account for other marketplace dynamics.
5. Consider unconventional pricing structures.

Estimate the Product's Dollarized Value

First you must understand the economic value your new offering delivers to your target customer. The value created by every unit of your offering establishes the dollarized price ceiling for your offering (represented by "a–d" in Figure 14.1). For example, if you are introducing a tool that eliminates $50 in labor costs, your price ceiling for that tool would be $50. Any price up to $50 would create a positive economic return for the customer.

Compare the Dollarized Value to the Price Floor

The total dollarized value provides an initial snapshot of your potential pricing window. You must next compare that value to the minimum price you would accept for the new product offering ("c–d" in Figure 14.1). This price floor is constructed by evaluating the direct cost of producing and delivering each unit,

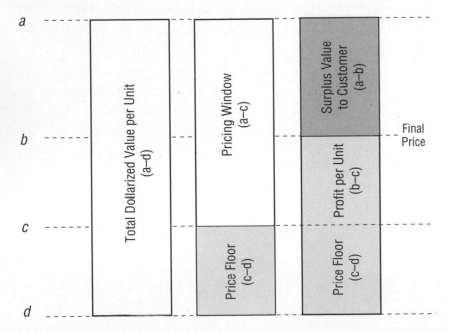

FIGURE 14.1   Factors to Consider in New Product Pricing

plus a minimally acceptable markup that would generate an acceptable contribution to your business.

If the total dollarized value per unit (a–d) is *less* than the price floor (c–d), the marketer must conclude that the product is economically unviable.

If instead the total value per unit does indeed exceed the marketer's acceptable price floor, the next task is to determine how far above that floor the marketer can manage to price the offering.

Consider the Target Customer's Investment Criteria

In the tool example, a $50 price would result in the following theoretical outcome: The customer could either pay $50 for a tool and save $50 on labor costs or spend $50 on labor and not buy the tool. The net economic outcome for the customer is the same either way. In effect, by purchasing the tool for $50, the customer is taking money out of one pocket and putting it in the other. The customer is no better off with or without the tool.

In order to be enticed to buy, the customer will demand to keep some of the incremental value created by the new product. The amount kept must satisfy the customer's investment criteria for making the outlay for the price of the product.

Different businesses set investment criteria differently. In the automotive industry, tight capital supply has resulted in a mandatory one-year payback requirement for any new capital investment. Other companies establish a rule-of-thumb hurdle rate to govern which projects or purchases are acceptable.

Hurdle Rate   The required rate of return on an investment, above which the investment makes sense and below which it does not.

For example, if the hurdle rate of your target customer group is 10 percent and your tool produces $50 in dollarized savings, you might calculate your target price this way:

Hurdle Rate = 10%

Gross Return on Investment = $50

$$\frac{\text{Gross Return} - \text{Price}}{\text{Price}} = \text{Return on Investment (ROI)}$$

$$\frac{\$50 - \text{Price}}{\text{Price}} = 10\%$$

Solving for price: $50 = 1.1 × Price; Price = $50/1.1 = $45.45

At a price of $45.45, the customer will earn a net return of $4.545, which is a 10 percent return on the investment of $45.45. A price of $45.45 or less would meet this customer's investment criterion.

Whatever the customer's method for evaluating the attractiveness of an investment, you must understand it and account for it in your pricing strategy.

Account for Other Marketplace Dynamics

After taking into account an acceptable return on investment for the customer, your pricing ceiling will land somewhere below point "a" in Figure 14.1. Next, you must evaluate other market dynamics that might influence where your final price will be. Dozens of factors come into play here, but some of the common considerations are discussed in the following pages.

How Defensible Is Your Competitive Advantage?

Often, a company will introduce a new product with new value-creating capabilities only to have competition match or surpass it within weeks or months. When market intelligence tells you this will be the case, it will likely influence how you approach your value-based pricing.*

Consider the following scenario. You have determined through careful dollarization analysis and by considering your customer's hurdle rate that your target price would be $50. The prevailing market price for this type of product is $30, and you now expect your toughest competitor to introduce a product similar to yours in six to nine months. Given this scenario, you might consider lowering your price to provide further financial incentive for your customers to purchase your new offering. For example, you might choose to lower your target price to $40 or thereabouts.

This could help in several ways: It would create a more robust ROI for customers, helping accelerate market penetration, giving you faster market share gains in advance of a competitive counterattack. It would also establish your price at a level that would leave the competitor little room to undercut you with drastically lower pricing. If the competitor were to offer a dramatically lower price, it would bump into conventional market prices, which presumably would undermine the competitor's own interest in gaining new pricing power with a new product.

What Is the Conventional Market Price?
While traditional cost-plus pricing is truly irrelevant if a new product offers significant improvements in economic value

---

*Another strategy to consider when a competitive response is anticipated is something we call the "window of opportunity" strategy. Detailed in Chapter 5, this strategy involves an *intentional* price step-down over time to counter the inevitable response from competition.

How Smart Are Your Competitors?

Price is a dangerous weapon when placed in the wrong marketer's hands. Every company has competitors, but all are not created equal. Companies that are fortunate enough to have smart competitors when it comes to pricing are blessed. Too often, we see smart companies that focus on the value they create for customers undermined by ignorant competitors that counter any marketplace challenge by cutting price. Robert Dolan and Hermann Simon observe, "Unless a firm has a very high level of product differentiation, its own profits are to some extent under the control of its competitors."[4]

What these price-cutters ignore is that a singular focus on cheap prices drives down profits for *all* players in an industry. As President William McKinley once proclaimed:

I do not prize the word cheap. It is not a badge of honor . . . it is a symbol of despair. Cheap prices make for cheap goods; cheap goods make for cheap men; and cheap men make for a cheap country!

While competition will drag down your ability to price high, disciplined differentiation and dollarization will help counter that drag on profits.

delivered, emotional responses from customers cannot be ignored. It is not uncommon for a customer, in the face of dramatically higher price points, to feel that a supplier is gouging. This is especially true when the buyer has deep experience with the product and has a solid understanding of what goes into making the product. A customer who knows a product costs pennies or dollars to make will emotionally resist paying a price that is a high multiple of that cost. Usually the reaction hinges on the customer's view of fairness. The customer might believe such a high price amounts to extortion, and, in response, might threaten to take the next opportunity to punish the supplier. Now, recognizing that a buyer's take on fairness will tend to focus on his or her own interests, it does make sense for a marketer to exercise prudence in these situations.

Again, the competitive marketplace will generally dampen the marketer's ability to price exorbitantly. The threat of newly emerging competitive offerings will prevent marketers from being too greedy. But given the chance, the marketer must balance the ability to price to full value against the potential emotional response of the customer.

In addition, there are sound economic reasons for such restraint. A price that is significantly higher than the market norm creates an increased economic incentive for competitors to improve their offerings. By introducing a new product that is even partially comparable to the high-priced, high-value product, the competitor is able to price below the market leader but still earn higher than average profit margins.

How Homogeneous Is the Market?

In some markets and product areas, the value delivered by a product is relatively constant from one customer to the next. For example, a lightbulb that saves electricity will save the same amount of electricity for every customer over the life of the bulb. Electricity rates may differ from one region to another, but a reasonable savings model can be built that is relevant for all consumers. In contrast, a washing machine that saves electricity and water will be viewed very differently by the family with five children than it will be by the working couple with no children and a dry-cleanable wardrobe.

The challenge for the marketer is to determine a pricing level that will provide a compelling enough value story for a large enough slice of the potential market without leaving too much money on the table with the high-use segment. This type of challenge can often be overcome by clever segmentation and segment-specific product offerings. But in many cases, the marketer must make trade-offs to find the sweet spot of a market.

Consider Unconventional Pricing Structures

Once you have established a target price, then it is time to get creative with how you *present* the price. If you anticipate emotional customer resistance because of a long-standing comfort with and awareness of market pricing, look for ways to unbundle your pricing. This can involve charging for use (rental) instead of a one-time price. It could involve charging one stripped-down price for the core product, and then charging extra fees for other components of the offering. For example, some companies charge special handling fees, odd-lot fees, engineering surcharges, environmental fees, and so on.

NEW PRODUCT PRICING EXAMPLES

The MicroPure Systems and Headstrong Dipstick cases illustrate the application of dollarization in the pricing of new products.

MicroPure Systems

MicroPure Systems* developed a patented technology for an electronic device that sanitizes water in closed industrial water systems, killing bacteria and other organisms that ordinarily contaminate such systems. The system also helps control scale buildup, the physical accumulation of minerals that can foul the workings of equipment.

MicroPure conducted preliminary evaluation work to transfer its industrial technology to a new market: the commercial swimming pool market. The technology promised commercial pool operators the opportunity to reduce a major operating cost—chlorine use—by two-thirds or more.

MicroPure's marketing team conducted a thorough evaluation of the marketplace. Part of the research focused on the potential economic impact of the pool sanitization system. Based on the research findings, MicroPure developed a pricing model based entirely on the system's dollarized value, without consideration for the cost of manufacturing the system.

The first challenge was to determine the typical chlorine usage for a commercial pool. While this appeared to be a straightforward task, the information proved evasive. Most pool operators are not aware of how much chlorine they use on a regular basis, or what their chlorine-related operating expenses are. In addition, the people responsible for hands-on operation of commercial swimming pools usually do not bear budgetary responsibility for chlorine costs, and are often not involved in the purchase of a maintenance item such as chlorine (this responsibility usually falls on the business office). Meanwhile,

---

*The name MicroPure Systems has been substituted to protect the confidentiality of the company discussed in this case study.

the business office often has little knowledge of the day-to-day operations of the pool. While nearly all pool operators expressed interest in the proposition of reducing chlorine usage by two-thirds, few were able to quantify what that savings would mean for their facility.

Most pool operators also believe that actual chlorine use depends on a variety of factors (temperature, bather load, etc.), which, they report, prevents them from being able to report a "typical" chlorine usage number. While chlorine use does indeed fluctuate with those factors, that variation could be dealt with. Further technical research discovered a formula developed by a major chlorine and chlorinating equipment manufacturer. The purpose of the formula was to estimate chlorine use for various pool types, accounting for indoor/outdoor variations, bather load, and other variables. The chlorine use formula proved to be the cornerstone in the development of the MicroPure value pricing model.

The formula provided a range of chlorine usage based on the size of a commercial pool (in gallons). Thus, MicroPure could conservatively estimate how much chlorine would be consumed by commercial pools of various sizes.

For example, a typical indoor lap pool (25 yards long with 6 lanes) holds approximately 120,000 gallons of water (depending on depth). This size pool would consume approximately 2.5 pounds of chlorine each day. At a market price of $2 per pound, chlorine usage for this pool would cost $5 per day or $150 in a typical month. Based on MicroPure's estimate of a two-thirds reduction in chlorine use, its system would save the operator of a 120,000 gallon pool $100 per month (2/3 × $150).

MicroPure also assessed the investment criteria of pool operators, and learned that an 18-month payback for a new investment was considered attractive. They also estimated that a pool operator would incur one-time costs of approximately $200 during the installation of the MicroPure sanitizing system. Gathering all this information, MicroPure priced the product as illustrated in Table 14.1.

This model produced a price that would generate 100 percent payback in 18 months, after which the value of the monthly chlorine savings went straight to the customer's bottom line.

The company developed system configurations appropriate for common commercial pool sizes (health clubs, hotels, universities) and established a price schedule covering each based on the calculations shown in Table 14.1.

The company also discovered that different customer segments approached purchasing with different mind-sets. For example, colleges and universities reported that they had an easier time getting approvals for one-time expenditures than they did when requesting increases to operating expense budgets, which were tight and carefully scrutinized. Hotel operators, on the other hand, could find operating expense money without much trouble, but faced an onerous process when requesting capital expense approval. In response, MicroPure developed pricing models to accommodate both. The company would offer colleges a one-time price ($1,600 in Table 14.1),

TABLE 14.1 MicroPure Pricing Calculations

Monthly Chlorine Use	$150
× Percentage Savings Produced by MicroPure System	66.7%
= Monthly Savings	$100
× 18 Months	$1,800
− Installation Costs	$200
= Pricing Target	**$1,600**

while it would offer hotels a "rental" agreement, where the customer essentially paid for the system out of the savings it generated.

Headstrong Dipstick

When we were first approached by the Headstrong Company* to help dollarize the value of a dipstick, we were a bit incredulous. But on further review, this seemingly prosaic product created value at every turn. The product was a dipstick and tube molded from a high-tech plastic. Its many novel features provided direct benefits to the truck engine makers that specified it, as well as other benefits to the ultimate operators of those trucks (which created marketing benefits for the truck engine makers).

The dipstick featured improved connections at the engine and at the cap, which prevented common "blow-by" leaks caused by elevated oil pressures. It also locked firmly in place and never shook loose due to engine vibration, a common problem with metal dipstick assemblies. Due to its size and shape, the plastic dipstick was easier to replace by the operator, and because it was plastic, not metal, it was never hot to the operator's touch. Cosmetically, the clean lines of the new dipstick were a big improvement over the ancient look of the metal dipsticks of yesteryear.

Inside the engine maker's plant, the dipstick was easier to assemble, saving up to 40 seconds per engine. It also enabled the truck maker to consolidate part numbers and eliminate 77 ac-

---

*The name Headstrong Company has been substituted to protect the confidentiality of the company discussed in this case study.

TABLE 14.2 Headstrong Dipstick Three-Year Summary

	Year 1	Year 2	Year 3
Total Dollarized Savings	$1,600,000	$1,200,000	$1,200,000
÷ Total Units	160,000	160,000	160,000
= Savings per Unit	$10	$7.50	$7.50

tive parts. In addition, it eliminated line stoppages caused by inaccurate assembly of the old design.

When all the various benefits were dollarized and totaled, the total benefit to one engine maker was $1,200,000 per year, plus an additional $400,000 in first-year savings. A summary of the dollarization analysis is provided in Table 14.2.

This analysis become the basis for the Headstrong team's pricing model (see Table 14.3). Note that the team used the lower year 2 and year 3 savings per unit as the basis for this analysis. This was done to provide the customer an extra savings incentive in year 1, as well as to present a more conservative, believable analysis.

The actual total cost per unit for the old dipstick ($13.50) became the price ceiling for the Headstrong team. Any price for the new product that was less than $13.50 would provide a net savings to the customer. Headstrong selected a price that would

TABLE 14.3 Headstrong Pricing Model

	Cost per Unit
Extra Cost per Unit of Continuing with Old Dipstick Design (from Table 14.2)	$7.50
+ Average Price of Old Dipstick	$6.00
= Actual Total Cost per Unit of Old Dipstick	$13.50

TABLE 14.4   Savings per Unit

Actual Total Cost per Unit of Old Dipstick	$13.50
– Price for New Dipstick	$9.00
= Net Savings per Unit for New Dipstick	**$4.50**

TABLE 14.5   Return on Incremental Investment

Net Savings per Unit for New Dipstick	$4.50
÷ Incremental Investment to Purchase New Dipstick ($9 – $6)	$3.00
= Return on Incremental Investment	**150%**

TABLE 14.6   Net Savings as Percentage of Current Price

Net Savings per Unit for New Dipstick	$4.50
÷ Average Price of Current Dipstick	$6.00
= Net Savings as a Percentage of Current Price	**75%**

fall midway between the old price and the total cost per unit for the old product.

- At $9.00, the new Headstrong dipstick provided net savings of $4.50 per unit (see Table 14.4).

- That savings represented an ROI of 150 percent to the customer (see Table 14.5).

- And in response to continuing price pressure from customer purchasing groups, Headstrong also demonstrated that the new dipstick program generated an effective 75 percent price reduction when all costs were considered (see Table 14.6).

Chapter 15

Dollarization and Market Segmentation

Market segmentation describes the division of a market into discrete homogeneous groups that will respond differently to promotions, communications, advertising, and other marketing mix variables. Segmentation is used by marketers to make marketing investments more efficient. Proper segment selection and an understanding of each segment's unique dynamics are critical in shaping marketing strategy.

Traditional segmentation approaches consider demographics, psychographics, Standard Industrial Classification (SIC) code analysis, and other readily available data-driven differentiators. Usage habits and other more qualitative measures are also used. This section reviews how dollarization analysis can also be helpful in optimizing segment selection.

One of the trade-offs in any pricing strategy is the choice between a "skimming" strategy and a "penetration" strategy. Price skimming occurs when the marketer prices a product at sufficiently high levels that large portions of a market find the price economically unacceptable. The slice of the market that *does* buy has different needs that permit the product offering to

159

deliver a dollarized value high enough to justify the high price. Thus, the marketer skims profits from the subset of the market that is willing to pay a premium price.

At the other extreme is penetration pricing, which occurs when the marketer acknowledges that some members of the target market will pay a higher price, but intentionally chooses a lower price point in order to attract a broader buying audience.

In both cases, the marketer's profits are suboptimal. Selling to fewer customers at a higher price forgoes any and all profit from customers who do not buy. Selling at a lower price forgoes the extra profits the marketer would earn from those customers who perceive the product's full value potential.

Perhaps the best possible scenario is when the marketer is able to customize prices for each and every customer on a case-by-case basis.

> Conceptually, the "best" way to price any new product is in terms of the value it contributes to a buyer. This approach, however, is feasible only when price discrimination among uses is possible.[1]

This approach is possible with product and service offerings that are specifically tailored for each customer or when the flow of information about market pricing is such that comparison shopping is not a threat.

Absent the ability to fully customize pricing, the next best alternative for the marketer is to use dollarization analysis to segment customers according to the value they receive and their willingness to pay.

> A product will often have a much higher perceived value for an "ideal" customer than for an average prospect. If this is

the case, a company would do well to separate the markets or segments and charge different prices accordingly.[2]

SEGMENTATION EXAMPLES

The following examples illustrate how companies have used dollarization in shaping their segmentation strategy.

Example 1

A leading elevator service company recently used its understanding of how various customers perceive the value of elevator service to create a three-tiered product scheme that enabled it to offer solutions to match customer value perceptions.

The first segment identified was price sensitive and placed low value on elevator maintenance. These customers saw elevator service as a necessary evil. Any attempt at dollarizing the value of elevator service was met with indifference. This customer group simply wanted minimal service at a minimum price. The service company offered these customers a solid, but bare-bones, service package that would meet their minimal needs at a market-competitive price point.

Another group of customers was similarly price conscious, but was somewhat willing to pay extra for fast service response. These customers understood that nonworking elevators created extra costs for their businesses (which could be dollarized), and were willing to pay for the security of guaranteed service. These customers were offered a base package, with several optional enhancements, including guaranteed service response times, for which they would pay extra.

The third group of customers saw elevator maintenance as critical to the operating success of their businesses. As a result, they were willing to pay for immediate service response, wanted access to maintenance and performance data, and welcomed other service enhancements. These customers were offered a comprehensive package that reflected the value they gained from preventive, diagnostic, and corrective elevator care.

Example 2

When Matrix Pipe Corporation* introduced the first flexible gas piping for residential construction, the company initially planned a broad-based market launch, with a standard product-centric message for all audiences. But as it began to test its messages in the marketplace, it learned that the different constituencies involved valued the product quite differently. The product, branded Sidewinder, replaced conventional black iron pipe. Sidewinder was flexible, weighed less, required fewer joints, and was easier and faster to install. Matrix marketing people conducted extensive research in the marketplace and redefined the key economic drivers for each potential segment.

Matrix learned that builders preferred Sidewinder because it accelerated home construction, reduced labor costs, and allowed them to add high-profit upgrades (such as gas fireplaces) at much lower costs. The speed improvement was the most important driver, as it allowed a builder to finish and sell a home faster. Part of Matrix's marketing pitch to builders included the line, "If time is money, Sidewinder is pure gold."

Gas utilities were another important target segment. Gas company growth is inherently limited by the number of residences connected to a company gas line. A key growth lever for

---

*The name Matrix Pipe Corporation has been substituted to protect the confidentiality of the company discussed in this case study.

these companies is maximizing the value of each customer hookup. Because Sidewinder made retrofit installation economically feasible, a customer whose gas usage was limited to, say, hot water heating might consider adding other applications (see Figure 15.1). The gas company could thereby increase its average revenue per customer connection.

The economic appeal to the people who install gas pipe (primarily plumbers) was a bit trickier. Because plumbers often charge by the hour, a product that would reduce the time required to complete a job was received with skepticism by many plumbing contractors. Instead, Matrix focused on other aspects of Sidewinder that created value (see Figure 15.2). For example, black iron pipe required a threaded joint at every turn, and each joint represented a potential leak path. Sidewinder, meanwhile, could be run for more than 100 twisty-turny feet with only a single

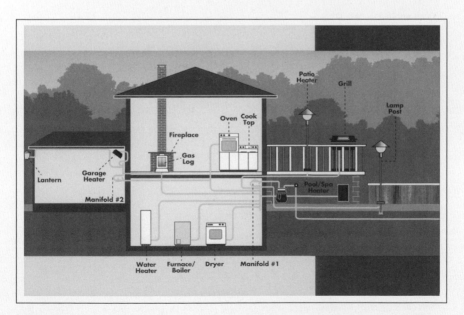

FIGURE 15.1 Marketing Sidewinder to Gas Utilities

FIGURE 15.2   Marketing Sidewinder to Plumbers

connection at either end. This appealed to plumbing contractors, because potential leaks mean potential uncompensated callbacks, where the plumber is called back to inspect and repair past work. In addition, Matrix sold plumbing contractors on the benefit of Sidewinder's light weight. Whereas with black iron pipe two people were needed for installation, Sidewinder's light weight enabled a single installer to lift 250 feet of pipe. One-man installation enabled the contractor to save on the cost of installing Sidewinder, while also freeing up an employee to work on another revenue-producing job.

Example 3

A leading maker of instant adhesives used dollarization to segment customer groups and to develop products suited for each segment. Because the company's base adhesive was versatile, it could be effectively used for many applications with little reformulation. The company would review potential customer uses and package and price the product according to the value delivered for each use. For example, one formulation was positioned for the repair of fine china. The company learned that a home-maker would be willing to pay a multiple of the price of general household adhesive to ensure that a $40 plate could be repaired and safely returned to the dining room table.

Example 4

Another interesting segmentation example relates to the Aloft bearing example detailed in Chapter 7. In reviewing its dollarization work with target customers, the Aloft marketing team discovered that coastal and island-based airlines expressed markedly higher interest than did inland airlines. The presence of moisture and sea air apparently accelerated corrosion for these airlines, making it a preventive maintenance priority. In response to this discovery, the marketing team refocused its efforts on selected coastal and island-based airlines, leaving the inland airlines for later. (The previous prioritization approach looked only at the size of a target customer fleet.) In addition, the marketer presented the corrosion resistance to the coastal airlines as a preventive measure, while it sold the corrosion resistance to inland airlines as a solution to a discrete but limited problem.

Chapter 16

Dollarization in Consumer Marketing

Dollarization works in nearly all business-to-business marketing and sales situations because businesses are implicitly profit-driven enterprises. The impact of any product or service investment by a business can be directly or indirectly linked to the company's financial performance. When marketing to consumers, dollarization must be used more selectively.

As we discussed in Chapter 2, people buy for two reasons: to feel good or to solve a problem (or both). As a rule, feel-good purchases cannot be dollarized. These purchases may create "psychic income" for customers, but they create nothing that can be deposited in the bank.

The solution to any business problem can always be dollarized. But solutions to consumer problems are somewhat ambiguous. In some cases, the solution to a consumer problem can be readily dollarized, but in many other cases, it cannot (see Table 16.1).

From Table 16.1, it is evident that the best opportunities for dollarizing consumer offerings involve products or services that directly impact other current expenditures. For example, Dryel

TABLE 16.1   Feel-Good versus Dollarized Purchases

Feel-Good Purchases	Dollarized Purchases
• Fine wine (tastes great). • Clothing (looks stylish, feels comfortable).* • Perfume and cologne (smell nice).* • Stereo system (has rich sound).	• Estate plan (avoids taxes). • New windows (saves heating costs). • Compact fluorescent lightbulb (saves electricity, needs replacement less often). • Reliable car (saves repair costs).

*See sidebar on beauty.

Dry Clean Only fabric care claims to be the "affordable alternative to dry cleaning." For 60 cents per garment, Dryel will handle a cleaning chore that otherwise might cost $3 or more at a professional dry-cleaning establishment.

We have yet to see it, but a related approach might come from a purveyor of wrinkle-free dress shirts, which enable men to avoid the $1.75 per shirt laundering charge at the local cleaner each time the shirt is worn.

One particularly challenging dollarization issue is when a product helps a consumer save *time*. Across the consumer marketing landscape, companies are introducing products and services that seek to exploit the frantically overscheduled lives many consumers lead. Products and services promise to free up "valuable time" so consumers can focus on activities that hold greater importance. But placing a monetary value on "valuable time" is in itself a challenge. Economists have struggled for years with models to accurately describe the

What Is Beauty Worth?

We would be the first to dismiss most attempts to dollarize the value of beauty-enhancing products. But a study by University of Texas economist Daniel Hamermesh has proven us wrong. The study, titled "Dress for Success—Does Primping Pay?," examined how a woman's investment in beauty-enhancing goods and services affected the woman economically. The study found that "beauty raises women's earnings (and to a lesser extent, men's) adjusted for a wide variety of controls." Further, the study found that investments in beauty pay back "at most 10 percent" in the form of higher earnings.

This might be a difficult way to sell cosmetics, but it does present one instructive lesson: Academic studies by economists are replete with obscure behavioral studies. Many a marketer can gain new insight by searching such papers for lessons relevant to the marketer's target customer group.

monetary value of a person's leisure time. Traditional models focus on an individual's income to impute an hourly worth for nonwork time. But these models fall down for several reasons, as articulated recently in the *Wall Street Journal*: "For instance, many people on a fixed salary do not have the option of getting extra pay if they work another hour. In addition, some people's work is keeping a house running, which doesn't come with a salary."[1]

The conclusion of the *Wall Street Journal* article is a set of calculations to help consumers analyze whether certain activities are worth an investment of their time. Those calculations look at the "cost" of doing a task, which is calculated by taking the sum of the income-based value of an individual's time plus the investment in tools and supplies required to complete the task. This is compared to the cost of hiring someone else to do the task. The results are then adjusted by a qualitative scoring of "psychological costs and benefits" (opportunity costs, enjoyment of task, ability to perform task, and indirect rewards). The calculation approach reflects the reality that nonfinancial factors must be weighed along with the imputed value of personal time based on employment income. The *Wall Street Journal* describes the limitations this way: "For many families the numbers are just a starting point. You can temper the equations with what economists call 'psychic variables.'" In other words, feel-good factors are implicit in valuing a consumer's time. This makes pure dollarization impossible in all but limited situations.

So while placing a value on consumer time may be difficult, many other consumer benefits *can* be dollarized. Figures 16.1, 16.2, and 16.3 are examples of consumer dollarization in action.

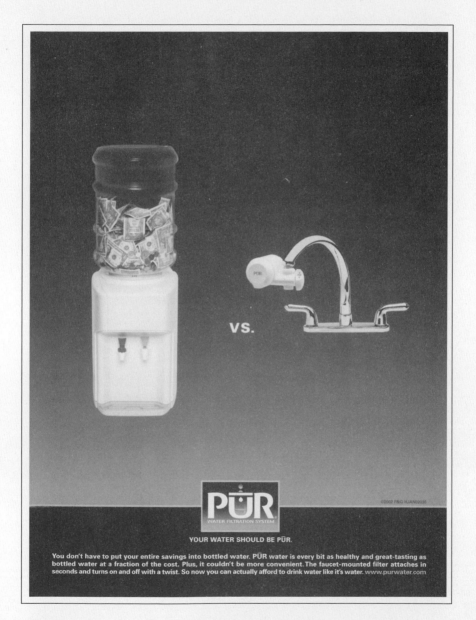

FIGURE 16.1   Recognizing the huge demand for pure bottled water, the marketers for PŪR water filtration system ran this advertisement positioning the PŪR filter as an affordable way to get the great taste of bottled water.

"Sometimes do-it-yourself doesn't pay."	
8 buckets of sealer	$ 80.00
Squeegee	$ 4.00
Oil stain prep seal	$ 6.00
New mat for trunk of car where sealer leaked	$ 40.00
Repaint car where cat walked	$350.00
Clean sealer off sidewalk, steps, and front porch	$ 50.00
Remove sealer and repaint front door and garage door	$ 80.00
New living room carpet	$800.00
Reseal driveway after lost driver turns around and kids play on it	$ 80.00
Doctor's bill, coal tar burns (when sealer comes in contact with skin)	$100.00
Reseal driveway (after rain washes away second coat)	$ 80.00
New shoes	$ 30.00
New shirt	$ 25.00
New pants	$ 20.00
New socks	$ 3.00
Hand cleaner and aspirin	$ 3.00
Chiropractic bills (after lifting heavy buckets of sealer)	$ 1,500.00
Divorce settlement	$20,000.00
TOTAL "DO-IT-YOURSELF COST"	$23,251.00

FIGURE 16.2 A clever local advertisement for the Armorseal Driveway Sealing service uses dollarization and humor to call attention to the hidden costs and potential hassle factor of do-it-yourself driveway sealing.

THE ATWOOD VS. STAYING AT HOME

Current Monthly Expenses		*Projected Monthly Expenses at The Atwood*	
Rent or Mortgage Payment	_____	Monthly Fee	_____
		(depending on the living accommodations you are considering)	
Utilities		Utilities	
• *Electricity*	_____	• *Electricity*	*$0*
• *Oil/Heating*	_____	• *Oil/Heating*	*$0*
• *Gas*	_____	• *Gas*	*$0*
• *Water*	_____	• *Water*	*$0*
• *Sewer*	_____	• *Sewer*	*$0*
Security	_____	Security	*$0*
Transportation	_____	Transportation	_____
Upkeep of Residence		Upkeep of Residence	
• *Lawn Care*	_____	• *Lawn Care*	*$0*
• *Painting*	_____	• *Painting*	*$0*
• *Plumbing*	_____	• *Plumbing*	*$0*
• *Exterior Maintenance*	_____	• *Exterior Maintenance*	*$0*
• *Landscaping/Seasonal Maint.*	_____	• *Landscaping/Seasonal Maint.*	*$0*
• *Snowplowing*	_____	• *Snowplowing*	*$0*
• *Condominium Maint. Fee*	_____	• *Condominium Maint. Fee*	*$0*
• *Other*	_____	• *Other*	*$0*
Linen Service	_____	Linen Service	*$0*
Housekeeping Services	_____	Housekeeping Services	*$0*
Restaurant Dining	_____	Restaurant Dining	_____
Health Club Membership	_____	Health Club Membership	*$0*
Property Taxes	_____	Property Taxes	*$0*
Homeowner's Insurance	_____	Residence Insurance	_____
Long-Term Health Care Insurance	_____	Long-Term Health Care Insurance	*$0*
TOTAL CURRENT MONTHLY EXPENSES	_____	**PROJECTED MONTHLY EXPENSES**	_____

Also consider these unanticipated items:
Roof Repair/Replacement, Furnace, Driveway, etc.

FIGURE 16.3 Faced with price-resistance, a community developed this side-by-side cost comparison to demonstrate the retirement dollarized savings a prospective resident could expect when moving from a private home.

Chapter 17

Dollarization and the Commodity Myth

When helping companies dollarize the value of their products, we often hear the lament: "Our customers care only about price. Our product is a commodity to them." Our standard response is to paraphrase Harvard Business School Professor Theodore Leavitt: "There is no such thing as a commodity, only lack of marketing imagination."

More specifically, there are two kinds of "commodity" companies: those that have differentiated offerings that are not understood, articulated, or defended, and those that need to find ways to differentiate their offerings.

But rather than dismiss the commodity myth, let's explore its roots and what can be done about it.

1. *Customers love commodities.* A commodity gives a customer the ultimate power to pit competitors against one another. This enables the buyer to secure the lowest price possible, even a price that is unprofitable to the seller.

2. *Because I said so!* Professional buyers will do everything in their power to make sellers believe their products are

commodities. Buyers are even given the "commodity buyer" *title* as a ploy to intimidate the seller. This has the effect of diminishing the sellers' will to fight for the reward for the value they might deliver.

3. *Sellers passively accept commodity status.* This happens for several reasons. First, sellers often lack information about their competitors' offerings, so they are unable to directly refute "commoditization" claims. Second, like schoolchildren who take everything their teachers say as gospel, sellers are often unwilling to question information given to them by customers. Third, sellers are often unaware of the full depth and breadth of their own offerings, and therefore are unable to demonstrate their differentiation. And fourth, some sellers subconsciously accept the customer's commodity stance because it frees them of the burden of professional selling responsibility. If the product is a commodity, they reason, then low price will win, and there is little a salesperson can do to change the outcome.

4. *Before dollarization must come differentiation.* By definition, a commodity product lacks differentiation and is interchangeable with other like commodities. It is true that it is impossible to dollarize *pure* commodities. But it is also true that very few products are *completely* interchangeable and *completely* without differentiation. It is the marketer's challenge to understand his areas of differentiation, and to look for new and creative ways to differentiate his offering.

The prolific Tom Peters had this to say about commodities (from www.TomPeters.com):

I recently got into a discussion about commodities with an engineer. He said his product was "becoming a commodity."

Before my next visit with him, I did a little market research. I purchased a four-roll package of one-ply generic toilet paper—an "obvious commodity"—at a cooperative grocery store. The price tag was 79 cents. Procter & Gamble's Charmin one-ply toilet paper, found in a nearby 7-Eleven store, had a $1.99 ticket. Both might appear to be the same product, "mere" one-ply toilet paper. Not so! The combination of Procter & Gamble's 150-year dedication to consumer quality and 7-Eleven's convenience led to $1.20 worth of value added onto the four-roll package that cost a quarter to produce.

So how do "commodity" marketers differentiate? They must first develop a thorough knowledge of their customers' needs and business drivers. This knowledge becomes the context filter for testing whether any newly developed differentiators will create meaningful value for a customer.

SEARCHING FOR
DIFFERENTIATION OPPORTUNITIES

In organizing a quest for differentiation, it is useful to rely on the traditional "Three Cs" of marketing: customers, competition, and company (see Figure 17.1).

WHAT TO DIFFERENTIATE?

Too many marketers focus narrowly on their core products when trying to differentiate. While never impossible, it may be difficult to find ways to differentiate certain mature products. However,

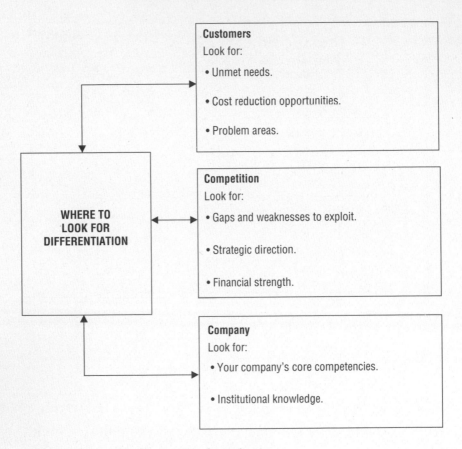

FIGURE 17.1 The Three Cs of Marketing

when a customer buys something, he is buying much more than the product itself. A perfect product at a great price is of little value if it doesn't arrive on time. And a great offering with no after-sales support may present unique difficulties for a company. Meanwhile, a perfect offering from a supplier that is teetering on the edge of bankruptcy brings with it other risks and associated costs.

When you begin to feel boxed in as a commodity, think expansively (see Figure 17.2).

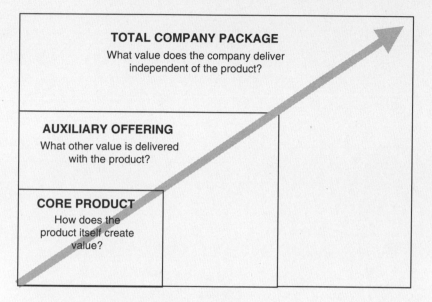

FIGURE 17.2 Routes to Differentiation

DIFFERENTIATING AND DOLLARIZING IN "COMMODITY" BUSINESSES

Following are examples of companies that escaped the commodity trap through differentiation and, ultimately, dollarization.

Example 1

An electric utility (which suffered the dual injustice of being both regulated *and* a commodity), founded a new, differentiated business based on an internal core competency it had developed. The firm had acquired unique expertise in the management and collection of utility receivables, and established an outsourcing business to sell that capability to other utilities (see more on this example in Chapter 10).

The company's sales pitch was pure dollarization:

The sooner we get started reducing ABC Utility's write-offs from 0.61 percent of revenue, the better. A 0.10 percent improvement adds over $2 million in free cash flow; that's $5,500 a day.

To achieve an equivalent bottom-line impact through utility rates would require a $13.3 million plant addition, assuming a 15 percent rate of return."

Example 2

A chemical maker faced down sure commodity status when a patent on a key chemical molecule expired. But rather than accept that fate, the chemical company developed a novel branded products strategy (see Figure 17.3), involving customized formulations for several niche markets. The company conducted exhaustive research to understand the usage requirements and other issues for each niche. This enabled the company to price and market each product according to the dollarized value it created for each niche (see Chapter 13 for more detail on this example).

Example 3

Most marketers would consider cardboard boxes a true commodity, but an innovative marketer of box partitions (the separators that keep wine bottles and other objects in place in a large carton) thought otherwise. It developed partitions that were fractions of an inch thinner than other available partitions, which

FIGURE 17.3 Niche Branding in the Chemical Industry

enabled their customers to buy smaller outer boxes, thus saving money on box costs. The space savings also created inventory and shipping savings for customers, which were not insignificant when multiplied by thousands of boxes.

Example 4

Despite actual technical differences among suppliers, many automotive companies have begun treating paint and coatings as commodities. Recognizing this dynamic, and also recognizing that the car companies would continue squeezing more and more service from the suppliers without extra pay, one leading supplier started a services business, which would sell services based on the technical expertise developed during its years as a supplier. The company used dollarization as a

cornerstone of its marketing strategy, introducing every program in the context of finding potential savings for its target
customer.

Example 5

A maker of carbide rods sold to the toolmaking industry believed it was selling a commodity, and its customers enthusiastically concurred. However, in-depth interviews with customers
and in-house technical experts uncovered small points of difference that would prove sufficient to gain a few extra wins in the
marketplace. The research revealed that this company's rods
were consistently rounder than competitive rods. Though the
difference was small, it produced measurable results when customers machined these rods into precision drills and other tools.
The customers were able to improve productivity and reduce
scrap, thus justifying the small premium the marketer had previously struggled to win.

Cool Cash for Truckers

Many operators of commercial trucks would dismiss engine coolants as an undifferentiated commodity. ChevronTexaco Global Lubricants, a leading provider of such products, believed otherwise. Its line of extended life coolants delivered several unique benefits to truck operators. The marketing challenge facing ChevronTexaco was the need to persuade its customers *and* its sales force that extended life coolant products were not, in fact, commodities but could create meaningful economic value for the end user.

The ChevronTexaco marketing team created a series of marketing tools to help pave the way for the sales force. They conducted in-depth research to understand the economics of fleet maintenance, and they also developed detailed performance data comparing their products to competitive offerings. The work demonstrated that the ChevronTexaco product could eliminate or drastically reduce many of the traditional costs associated with coolant maintenance, including materials and labor for testing, replacement of coolant, recharging, and disposal.

This work was packaged into professional presentation pieces, detailed cost calculators (see Figure 17.4), and a road map for introducing the product benefits in a way that would enable customers to see the specific savings available for their fleets (see Figures 17.5 and 17.6).

PM5

Texaco Extended Life Prediluted 50/50 Coolant
versus
Fully Formulated Coolant with Liquid SCAs
Coolant Maintenance Cost Comparison

Fully Formulated Coolant with Liquid SCAs — Total cost to use for a *single vehicle* for 6 years/600,000 miles or 12,000 hours of service	Texaco Extended Life Coolant Solution — Total cost to use for a *single vehicle* for 6 years/600,000 miles or 12,000 hours of service

A: Initial cost of 50/50 blend Coolant
12 (# of gallons) x $3.75 (cost per gallon) = $45.00

A: Initial cost of 50/50 blend Coolant
12 (# of gallons) x $6.00 (cost per gallon) = $72.00

B: Initial cost of SCA charge (liquid or filter)
$0.00 (cost of precharge) = $0.00

B: Initial cost of SCA charge (liquid or filter)
n/a (cost of precharge) = n/a

C: 6 year/600,000 mile cost of test kits or strips
30 (# of kits or strips) x $0.50 (cost per unit) = $15.00

C: 6 year/600,000 mile cost of test kits or strips
n/a (# of kits or strips) x n/a (cost per unit) = n/a

D: 6 year/600,000 mile labor cost incurred for testing
30 (# of tests) x 1/6 (# of labor hours) x $32.00 (Labor cost per hour) = $160.00

D: 6 year/600,000 mile labor cost incurred for testing
n/a (# of tests) x n/a (# of labor hours) x n/a (Labor cost per hour) = n/a

E: 6 year/600,000 mile cost of SCA recharges (liquid or filter)
30 (# of recharges) x $5.00 (cost per recharge) = $150.00

E: One time application cost of Texaco Extender at 300,000 miles.
1 (# of applications) x $8.00 (cost per application) = $8.00

F: 6 year/600,000 mile labor cost of SCA recharges (liquid or filter)
30 (# of recharges from E) x 1/6 (# of labor hours) x $32.00 (Labor cost per hour from D) = $160.00

F: One time application labor cost of Texaco Extender at 300,000 miles.
1 (# of applications from E) x 1/6 (# of labor hours) x $32.00 (Labor cost per hour) = $5.33

G: 6 year/600,000 mile cost of Coolant change-outs
$45.00 (Total from A:) x 2 (# of change-outs) = $90.00

G: 6 year/600,000 mile cost of Coolant change-outs
n/a (Total from A:) x n/a (# of change-outs) = n/a

H: 6 year/600,000 mile labor cost incurred for Coolant change-out
2 (# change-outs from G) x 1 (# of labor hours) x $32.00 (Labor cost per hour from D) = $64.00

H: 6 year/600,000 mile labor cost incurred for Coolant change-out
n/a (# change-outs from G) x n/a (# of labor hours) x n/a (Labor cost per hour) = n/a

I: 6 year/600,000 mile Coolant disposal costs
12 (# of gallons from A) x 2 (# change outs from G) x $0.75 (Disposal cost per gallon) = $18.00

I: 6 year/600,000 mile Coolant disposal costs
n/a (# of gallons from A) x n/a (# change outs from D) x n/a (Disposal cost per gallon) = n/a

J: Make-up / Top off Coolant cost
6 (# of years) x 5 (# of gallons) x $3.75 (cost per gallon from A) = $112.50

J: Make-up / Top off Coolant cost
6 (# of years) x 5 (# of gallons) x $6.00 (cost per gallon from A) = $180.00

K: The total cost of maintaining a single engine's coolant system for 6 years/600,000 miles or 12,000 hours using your existing coolant.
$814.50

K: The total cost of maintaining a single engine's coolant system for 6 years/600,000 miles or 12,000 hours using Texaco ELC Prediluted 50/50 Coolant.
$265.33

This is an estimate of how much you might save

Single Engine Savings 6 Years/600,000 miles

Total current coolant cost	−	Total Texaco ELC cost	=	Single Engine Savings
$814.50		$265.33		$549.17

Fleet Savings 6 Years/600,000 miles

Single Engine Savings	x	# of Fleet Vehicles	=	Fleet Savings
$549.17		100		$54,917

Labor Hours Savings 6 Years/600,000 miles

Total employee labor hours for current coolant	−	Total employee labor hours for Texaco ELC	=	Single engine employee labor hours savings
12.56		0.17		12.40

Labor hours = Total from D+F+H+I / $ Labor Rate

Fleet Labor Hours Savings 6 Years/600,000 miles

Single engine employee labor hours savings	x	# of Fleet Vehicles	=	Fleet Labor Hours Savings
12.40		100		1,239.58

This is how fast you could receive your Payout

Maintenance Costs	÷	Months	=	Avg maint cost / month		Texaco ELC Initial Fill Cost	÷	Avg maint cost / month	=	Months for Payout
$485.00		72		$6.74		$72.00		$6.74		10.69
Total from C+D+E+F		Months in 6 years								

These statements and estimations shown herein are not guarantees of future performance and are subject to certain risks, uncertainties and other factors, some of which are beyond our control and are difficult to predict. Therefore, actual outcomes and results may differ materially from what is expressed or forecasted in such statements and estimates. You should not place undue reliance on these forward-looking statements, which speak only as of the date of this earnings release. Unless legally required, ChevronTexaco undertakes no obligation to update publicly any forward-looking statements, whether as a result of new information, future events or otherwise.

A **ChevronTexaco** Product

FIGURE 17.4 ChevronTexaco salespeople use this detailed cost calculator to help customers calculate the savings that can be achieved by converting to extended life coolants from their current practice. The detailed inputs prompt the salesperson to ask diagnostic questions about the customer's current coolant maintenance practices.

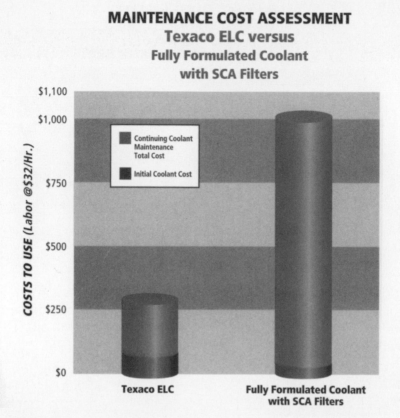

MAINTENANCE COST ASSESSMENT
Texaco ELC versus
Fully Formulated Coolant
with SCA Filters

FIGURE 17.5 This visual presentation of the cost comparison demonstrates how an incremental initial investment of just $27 generates more than $800 in maintenance savings over 6 years or 600,000 miles.

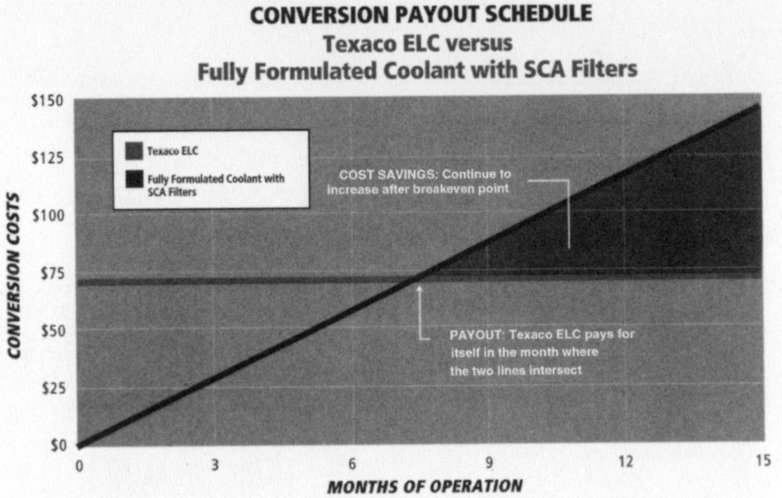

FIGURE 17.6 This payout chart shows the customer the time required to break even on the initial investment in converting a fleet to extended life coolants. After the "payout" point, all savings go directly into the customer's pocket.

Chapter 18

Dollarization and New Product Direction

We've looked at how dollarization can help when pricing a new product and when selling a new product to a customer. But long before a company gets to the pricing or selling stage, dollarization can play an important role in the new product conceptualization and development process. Specifically, the identification of opportunities to generate value for your customer can provide *inspiration* for new product development work. And during the new product validation stage, a critical criterion for testing a concept's ultimate marketplace viability is the product's ability to generate dollarized value for target customers.

DOLLARIZATION AND NEW PRODUCT IDEATION

Innovation in new products and services is a critical competency for any firm. Innovation is also a challenge for many firms, especially those that suddenly face the need to innovate after years of complacency. Based on a review of the literature, there is no shortage of potential processes and theories for these companies to try. One topic on which most experts will agree is that a company must cast a wide net when looking for innovation opportunities. Important tools a company should use in casting that net are its understanding of the economics of current customers, and the opportunities the company sees to enhance those economics.

> A knowledge of customers includes an understanding of their requirements as well as their economics. By looking at a product or service from the viewpoint of the customer and understanding its total cost of ownership and the way it creates value, a supplier can determine how existing or new offerings could help the customer add still greater value. Such "value selling" differs from the common costs-plus approach, which bases prices on the sum of cost components; it is instead based on creating, emphasizing, and capturing more of the economic value from a product or service for all downstream players. A supplier that takes this approach goes beyond its current catalog by inventing combinations of products and services and by suggesting outsourcing opportunities that meet each customer's long-term needs better than its competitors could.[1]

Innovation can come in all shapes and sizes, and need not relate directly to a change in a company's core product. Enhancements to the way the product is packaged, delivered, and serviced can also help companies create and recover incremental value with their customers. Truly breakthrough innovation, while exciting, is a rare business event. It is also a risky proposition, with many truly new products never achieving financial breakeven. Most successful innovation instead takes the form of relentless, incremental improvements to a company's existing offering.

Innovation ideas can come from company sales, service, and technical people, who see customer problems firsthand every day. They can also be discovered through other more formal means, including focus groups (and other customer research), best practices reviews, and brainstorming. But the intimacy of the day-to-day interaction between seller and customer provides a unique environment for generating new opportunities. Generally, there is already an established trust, and there exists some level of mutual understanding of each party's institutional competencies and shortcomings. When a seller plays a consultative role, focusing on the dollarized value it helps create for the customer, this further enhances the environment. A customer who believes the seller is truly seeking to improve the customer's business situation will be more agreeable to new ideas from the seller.

VALUE CREATION EXAMPLES

The following examples illustrate how sellers' understanding of their customers' economic drivers can help shape the development of new products and services.

Example 1

California Aerospace Sealants (CAS)* was traditionally a supplier of bulk sealants to aerospace companies. CAS sealants were regarded as the best available, but CAS continued to look for ways to grow through innovation. CAS would deliver its

---

*The name California Aerospace Sealants (CAS) has been substituted to protect the confidentiality of the company discussed in this case study.

product in drums, and the customer would take over from there (with CAS providing technical assistance as needed). As CAS people spent time in their customers' plants, they observed multiple issues. Customers would waste CAS product due to improper handling, measurement, and job planning. The product waste also created disposal costs, which were substantial given the hazardous classification of certain chemicals. Customers also worried about the proper application of the sealants, as the areas to be sealed were often blind to the customer employee and difficult to inspect (e.g., inside a tank).

CAS responded by delivering a series of packaging and product innovations. It developed single-use applicators, which enabled the customer to eliminate manual mixing, measuring, and handling. Essentially, a worker could pick up the number of applicators needed for a job and go right to work, without having to prepare the sealants. By using applicators, the customer also eliminated the not uncommon occurrence of disposing of half-full pails of mixed sealant. If workers overestimated the number of applicators needed, they would simply return the unused extras to the cabinet when finished.

In addition, CAS developed various types of "pre-formed" product—for example, they developed a pre-formed sealant cap that could be pushed onto the head of a bolt to seal it. The old method required using a brush or caulk gun to apply the sealant. In blind applications, these old approaches took much longer and risked missealing some of the intended locations. Sealant was also pre-formed into a tape that could be rolled onto long, thin surfaces to seal gaps, again saving the customer time in application, prep, and cleanup.

Each of these innovations was driven by an identified opportunity to create value for the customer and to share in that value creation. Each was also priced to reflect the value created.

Example 2

A leading maker of engineered components discovered that customers were continually asking for ideas to help them simplify the assembly of the components they purchased. The supplier obliged, adding alignment tabs and a variety of other discrete features to assist customers. The supplier understood that its customers were fighting offshore competitors with much lower cost structures for manual operations (such as assembly). It also understood that if its customers lost business to these low-cost competitors, it would lose business, too. Clearly, assembly speed and cost were a critical area of focus for these customers.

The component supplier determined that innovative tweaks to its components would take its customers only so far. It then embarked on a more holistic strategy. Because of its own in-house design, manufacturing, and assembly capabilities, the supplier figured it could take some of the assembly work off the customer's plate by selling preassembled modules comprised of multiple components. By taking the full responsibility under its own roof, the supplier was able to redesign parts, eliminate manufacturing costs, and stage the production and assembly so that the customer's total costs were slashed. The supplier also enhanced its own revenue and gross margin performance by sharing in the total value it helped create.

NEW PRODUCT VALIDATION

A new product must pass a full gauntlet of tests before it is ready for launch, including performance testing, customer acceptance, durability, manufacturability, and cost position. We would argue that a dollarization litmus test is as important as any of these other evaluations. If a new product offering will not deliver sufficient value to justify a customer investment, all the other performance measures are moot.

The following examples illustrate how dollarization validation can alter new product launch plans.

Example 1

MicroPure Systems was planning to introduce its electronic pool sanitizer to the commercial pool market. Its initial plan was to target all commercial pools, both indoor and outdoor. MicroPure's pricing model (see Chapter 14) was based directly on the dollarized value its system created for pool operators. The value was primarily generated by reducing a customer's chlorine usage by two-thirds.

During the validation of its pricing model, MicroPure conducted detailed research among pool operators and other industry experts. Despite the appeal of the outdoor pool market—commercial outdoor pools outnumber indoor pools by a factor of at least four to one, and the average outdoor pool is larger than the average indoor pool—the dollarized economics did not work. Outdoor pools, MicroPure learned, lose a great deal of chlorine to the effects of the sun. In addition, many outdoor pools are operated on a seasonal basis. These factors combined to make MicroPure's key economic driver, chlorine use reduction, marginal. MicroPure calculated the price an outdoor pool operator could justify paying for the new system. The value indicated a price that was unacceptably low to MicroPure. The company instead redoubled its focus on the indoor pool market, where the economics were robust.

Example 2

Piccadilly Tools* was preparing to launch a new "smart" wrench for securing lug nuts on automotive wheels. Piccadilly's marketing team had developed a complex dollarization model to demonstrate the new system's value, evaluating the cost of accidents caused by improperly fastened lug nuts, rework costs for the tire shop, and other customer-satisfaction-related values (see Chapter 21). During its final market testing, the team discovered a discrepancy that would shift its launch plans. The dollarization story held up for many of the large, national discount tire chains. These chains were characterized by high turnover in low-wage laborers, a recipe that led to quality control concerns for chain management. The smart wrench represented a mechanism for reducing the quality problems caused by the worker issues. However, there are also thousands of regional and locally owned tire shops that tend to keep a more stable, qualified class of technician. The management of these shops reported low frequency of lug-nut-related reworks, and expressed little concern about quality control problems. Local tire shops believed that Piccadilly's economic model did not apply to them, and therefore had little interest in the system. Piccadilly instead shifted its resources to launching the smart wrench to the large tire chains.

---

*The name Piccadilly Tools has been substituted to protect the confidentiality of the company discussed in this case study.

DOLLARIZATION TECHNIQUES

Never value the valueless. The trick is to know how to recognize it.
—Sidney Madwed
(Poet and business consultant)

Ask, and it shall be given you; seek, and ye shall find; knock, and it shall be opened unto you.

—Matthew 7:7

Chapter 19

The Mechanics of Dollarization

When a company decides to put dollarization to work in sales and marketing, there are three major disciplines that must be addressed. Each requires a different set of skills and each can be accomplished through a variety of approaches. However, a dollarization strategy that underinvests in any one of these activities will underperform.

DOLLARIZATION PROCESS STEPS

The three process steps are:

1. *Dollarization discovery.* Determine how your offering results in financial value to your customers.

    The outcome of this step is the arithmetic formulas required to calculate your dollarized value. The actual data needed to populate those formulas must be developed separately.

2. *Data development.* Develop the data required to calculate the dollarized value you deliver to customers.

This step enables you to complete the equations developed in the discovery phase with real numbers.

3. *Strategy integration.* Determine how to use your dollarized story to shape your marketing and sales approaches.

This is where dollarization is put to work to improve your business. Chapters 5 through 18 focus on this aspect of dollarization.

At first glance, it would seem logical that these steps must proceed neatly in sequence, one after the other. But in practice the sequence can shift, and in some circumstances the steps may occur more or less simultaneously.

Consider the following examples:

Example 1

The purest use of these steps tends to occur when a marketing professional seeks to shape strategy through a better understanding of the dollarized value of her offering, as illustrated in the following example.

1. *Discovery.* A product manager for a software firm conducts customer interviews, leads focus groups, and uses other market research tools to discover the mechanisms through which her offering creates value for customers:

Value-creating benefit. Software tool eliminates the need for training customer employees.

2. *Data development.* Once the value-creating mechanisms are discovered, the product manager follows up with more

focused research to discover the actual *values* needed to *dollarize* the benefits identified as value-creating:

Dollarization data development. The training that is eliminated by the marketer's software typically consists of 8 to 12 man-days of training per year, at a cost to the employer of $100 to $125 per man-day.

3. *Strategy integration.* Next the product manager must determine how to use this information in shaping the marketing strategy and execution plan for her product. This could involve several elements.

Strategic and executional direction. Armed with the knowledge gained in steps 1 and 2, the product manager can now:

- Position and brand the product as a "training cost eliminator."
- Price the product to reflect the value created (10 to 12 training days × $100 to $125 per day).
- Create a pricing structure based on the number of employees who will use the software.
- Create advertising messaging based on the savings.
- Create sales tools that enable salespeople to customize the analysis for customers.
- Train salespeople on how to sell the economic benefits of the software rather than just the technical features/benefits.

Example 2

In some cases, the marketer can jump from step 1 to step 3 while leaving step 2 for later. This can occur when the mecha-

nism for creating value is relatively consistent from one customer to the next, but the actual value created is specific to the
customer circumstances.

1. *Discovery.* Based on competitive product testing, a carbide
   metalworking tool salesperson is equipped with technical
   data demonstrating that his new drill will cut faster than
   competitive drills.

   Value-creating benefit. Drill allows customer to drill
   more parts per shift.

2. *Strategy integration.* The salesperson approaches his customer with the technical performance data and persuades
   the customer that the new tool is worthy of evaluation. He
   integrates this into his selling strategy as follows:

   Strategic and executional direction. The salesperson
   might set up his sales proposition this way:

   > Mr. Customer, we've agreed that this drill will cut faster
   > than the drill you are using now, and we've also acknowl-
   > edged that our pricing on the new drill is higher than
   > what you are paying for your current drill. Would you
   > agree that the logical next step is to test the drill in your
   > application to determine how much faster this drill will
   > cut in your process? If this testing demonstrates savings
   > in excess of the difference in price, are there any other is-
   > sues that would prohibit you from going with our drill?

3. *Data development.* Once the customer agrees to the testing
   and conditionally agrees to buy if the testing justifies the
   price difference, the salesperson can push ahead with a testing program to generate the data required to make that case.

   Dollarization data development. The testing demonstrates a 15 percent performance improvement, which re-

sults in savings of $750 per shift. The increased drill invest-ment is only $150 per shift, so the data justifies a switch to the new drill.

Example 3

In some cases—especially when the marketer's offering is engi-neered or tailored specifically for each customer—the "needs analysis" phase of face-to-face consultative selling might encom-pass all three steps.

For example, a salesperson might enter a conversation with an existing or prospective customer with a dollarization mind-set and proceed to probe for customer problems for which the seller's offering provides potential cures. In the course of that probing, the seller might discover the economic consequences of those problems (discovery), and if prepared and alert, might also discover the building-block data required to calculate the actual dollarized values (data development). Additionally, during the same visit, the salesperson might learn about the decision-making process at the target customer, and thereby gain insight as to how to use his dollarized story to shape his selling strategy (strategy integration).

SUMMARY

As stated previously, much of this book addresses the many strat-egy integration opportunities provided by dollarization:

Chapter 5:   Dollarization and Selling Your Price
Chapter 6:   Dollarization and Selling Something New

The next few chapters address more specifically how to approach the dollarization discovery and data development steps. Both of these steps can be accomplished by a variety of approaches. The balance of this book explains and illustrates the more common approaches.

Chapter 20

How to Dollarize Any Benefit

The act of translating a benefit into the financial gain it creates for a customer is mechanically straightforward, but it can at times be tricky. It requires a thorough understanding of your product's benefit set and of how your offering is different from the other options the customer might be considering. It also requires insight into the dynamics of your customer's business, and importantly, how your offering impacts those dynamics. And while some fundamental financial awareness is important, one does not need to be a certified public accountant (CPA) to put dollarization into practice.

Dollarizing your benefits sometimes requires creativity and keen insight into your customer's business. It may not always be precisely evident how a benefit leads to financial gain, but you must sleuth your way to an answer. Of course, asking your customer directly is the best first course of action. But customers do not always know the answers we seek. As an alternative, market research may be required to understand the potential financial impacts. But you can often find answers within your own company in the form of collective institutional experience with the target customer group. Unless you are introducing a product to an entirely new and unfamiliar marketplace, chances are good that there are colleagues in your firm who know your target customer dynamics pretty well.

If your firm's institutional knowledge *does not* include familiarity with your target customer group, internal resources can still be helpful. Various functional representatives at your company can act as a proxy for your customer in thinking through how to dollarize the benefits your company delivers to a customer. If, for example, you are perplexed about how a customer might view the impact of a delayed capital expenditure, your own finance department can provide insight. Or, if you are unclear how incremental productivity improvements in a customer's assembly plant create value, talk to a plant manager at your own company. Your own logistics team can shed light on how your customer thinks about his supply chain.

FIVE STEPS TO DOLLARIZATION

Whenever you start evaluating the value you create for a single customer or an entire population of customers, it is important that you methodically review all the potential impacts. Leave no stone unturned. Whatever sources you use to develop your understanding of the value created, the following steps will guide you.

1. *Determine who is your competition.* First, you must know what you are selling against. Is it a traditional industry competitor? Is it an internally developed solution? Is your competition the status quo? You must know what you are selling against before you can begin to dollarize. Often, you will need to dollarize against multiple enemies.

2. *Articulate your differentiating features.* When compared to the competition you are facing, what are the specific differentiating elements of your offering? Consider every element of your total offering, from the product itself, to the service package that comes with it, to your overall company picture. You must be precise and comprehensive in this assessment.

3. *State your benefit(s).* Next, you must identify all the ways your differentiating features benefit your customer. It is helpful to ask yourself the following questions, and to try to answer them from the customer's perspective:

   - How does this feature help the customer?
   - Why should the customer care about this feature?
   - What customer problems does this solve?
   - What are the consequences if the customer *does not* get this feature?

Note that it is not uncommon for the same feature to result in multiple customer benefits. For example, lighter airplane components could result in fuel savings, longer flight range, and/or higher cargo payload. In other cases, one benefit may create linked follow-on benefits. For example, improved reliability could result in lower warranty costs, and lower warranties could result in improved customer satisfaction, which could mean higher repeat sales. Be sure to think through the full effect of your value (see "The Ripple Effect" later in this chapter).

Also be careful to measure your benefits against the customer's actual needs and interests. Do not fall prey to marketing tunnel vision. Your benefits, as exciting as they are to you, may be meaningless to your customer (remember the long-lasting paint example in Chapter 1 when the customer was planning to sell his house).

4. *Quantify your benefit.* The next step is to determine how to quantify each benefit delivered by your product or service. This is where you convert benefit language into numbers. For example:

Words	Numbers
Yield improvement	40 grams more per batch
Reduces downtime	30 minutes of unplanned downtime per shift
Improved productivity	8 more units per hour
Better performance	3 percent gain in market share for customer

Occasionally the quantification step is a direct leap to dollars and cents, but typically, it is helpful to first develop a quantified measure of the direct benefit.

5. *Dollarize.* Finally, you must determine how the quantified benefit results in dollars-and-cents savings for the customer (see Table 20.1).

After you've worked through this five-step process, you will have drawn the connection between your offering and exactly how it creates value for your customer. You will not, however, have actually calculated that value. That step comes next.

Sometimes, in the course of executing the five steps outlined, you will also discover much of the data required to complete the analysis. But more often, these steps are a preparatory process that must be followed by a series of fact-finding steps. This fact-finding process is addressed in Chapter 21.

TABLE 20.1 Quantifying and Dollarizing Benefit Results

Words	Numbers	Dollars
Yield Improvement	40 Grams More per Batch	40 Grams × $100 per Gram = $4,000 per Batch
Reduced Downtime	30 Minutes of Unplanned Downtime per Shift	30 Minutes × $500 per Minute of Downtime = $15,000 per Shift
Improved Productivity	8 More Units per Hour	8 Units × $10 per Unit = $80 per Hour
Better Performance	3% Gain in Market Share for Customer	3 Share Points × $500,000 per Share Point = $1.5 Million

STAY FLEXIBLE

You may find that a single customer benefit can have very different dollarized values to different customers. This requires that you adapt your dollarization approach based on each customer's specific circumstances. Consider this example: Acme Electronics* sells a gadget that accelerates the assembly process in consumer electronics factories by 20 percent. Acme introduces this benefit to customer 1 and determines that the primary value lies in the reduction in labor costs. Customer 1 is thrilled with the potential labor savings.

Acme then enthusiastically approaches customer 2 with a similar labor savings pitch and customer 2 responds with ho-hum

---

*The name Acme Electronics has been substituted to protect the confidentiality of the company discussed in this case study.

interest in the labor cost savings. However, upon further review, Acme discovers that customer 2 is facing a capacity crunch. It is selling everything it can make, and its assembly process is the bottleneck. Customer 2 couldn't care less about labor costs; it simply needs to make more product! By improving assembly speed by 20 percent, Acme enables customer 2 to increase its overall output, increase its overall sales, and increase its profit generation. The dollarized value to customer 2 is 50 times greater than the value to customer 1.

THE RIPPLE EFFECT

When dollarizing any benefit, it is natural for a seller to rely on the interpretations of the customer contacts with which he works most intimately. But the views of those contacts may limit the seller's ability to see the full impact of a benefit.

The professional seller must be alert and investigative when working with a customer. Many of the benefits a seller delivers have a substantial ripple effect through the customer's business. Consider this example:

1. Seller improves the tolerance of a bearing to help a customer's engineering department achieve a design specification.
2. The improved tolerance reduces the noise produced in the customer's equipment.
3. The reduced noise eliminates the majority of complaints from the customer's customers.
4. The reduced noise also avoids Occupational Safety and Health Administration (OSHA) penalties for the customer's customer.

5. Ultimately, the customer is able to increase sales by 2 percent due to improved customer satisfaction.

The lesson to keep in mind is that you must always probe beyond the obvious benefit of your solution. This requires knowing your customer's business, knowing contacts throughout the organization, and asking excellent needs-analysis questions. Identify the real value and you will be rewarded for it.

Soft Costs = Soft Thinking

When working through the dollarization of your benefits, you may run into a concept known as the "soft cost." If customers resist aspects of your value analysis, stating that pieces of your calculated value represent soft costs, they are essentially claiming that the costs are not real. Soft costs *are* real, but they can be difficult to account for.

In some cases, soft costs are a challenge because traditional Financial Accounting Standards Board (FASB) accounting practices do not allow companies to directly measure them, which means company managers do not get direct credit for reducing them. Activity-based costing (ABC) can help measure specific impacts, but few companies actively use ABC to manage their businesses. But more often, soft costs become an issue because real cost impacts are not adequately thought through.

Perhaps the best example of a soft cost is when a product or service creates a productivity improvement for a customer. The productivity gain might allow a customer employee to complete a task 33 percent faster than before. Initially, the seller may calculate the dollarized impact as 33 percent of the worker's wages. The seller's logic goes like this:

(Continued)

Soft Costs = Soft Thinking *(Continued)*

If the customer's staff can be 33 percent more productive, then the customer will be able to reduce manpower costs by 33 percent while still generating the same production.

Meanwhile, the customer is thinking: Unless I eliminate a worker altogether, I still must pay the worker 100 percent of his or her wages, so a productivity gain, while positive, does not go directly to the bottom line (unless the productivity gain overcomes a production constraint and results in incremental revenue).

The thinking of both parties is legitimate, but flawed by a narrowness of scope. In these situations, understanding the dollarized value requires more expansive thinking. The customer may *not* be able to directly reduce payroll as a result of the productivity improvement, but might benefit in other areas. For example, the customer may be able to reduce or eliminate overtime pay that was necessary because prior to the productivity gain the regular workload could not be accomplished within the normal workday. Or, during periods of spike activity, the customer might be able to meet output demands that otherwise cause delays with related costs. Another possible outcome is that the customer workforce is able to complete its responsibilities at a less frenzied pace, which could improve quality, reduce warranty problems, and so on.

It may not be easy to peg a precise value in such soft cost situations, but before capitulating to the customer's claim of "no value," explore and probe for the real impact your contributions create.

Chapter 21

Developing Dollarization Data

Once the marketer has developed an understanding of the *mechanisms* by which her offering creates value for customers, she is faced with the challenge of actually quantifying and dollarizing that value.

The two key areas of information requiring development are:

1. Data that *quantifies* the performance advantage.
2. Data that *dollarizes* the quantified performance advantage.

Often, both of these discovery steps can be accomplished in the course of routine interaction with the customer, or the marketer will find that the required data can be developed quite fully through internal means, with just a few bits of data needed from external sources. But in many cases the data appears elusive, so the marketer must develop creative means to collect the necessary information.

The examples that follow illustrate various approaches available for developing dollarization data. It is important to note (as detailed in Chapter 22) that regardless of the source of data or the method of data collection, the marketer must carefully gain the customer's confidence that the data is indeed valid and appropriate for the customer's business situation. Without this agreement, data that shows millions of dollars in value may prove worthless.

DIRECT INTERVIEWS WITH THE CUSTOMER

When a company is selling products that are custom-engineered, services that are specifically tailored, or other offerings that are unique to each buying customer, the only feasible approach for developing applicable dollarization data is to pursue a direct, preferably collaborative approach with the target customer.

This type of data development responsibility tends to fall on the sales side of an organization, although product managers and other marketing resources are often involved as well. Because much of this work is done face-to-face (or by phone) with the customer, it requires careful training, practice, and diligent planning (for more on this, see Chapter 22).

Consider the following examples:

Example 1

A salesperson for a leading industrial seal manufacturer is working with a customer in the farm tractor market. The customer is having failure problems with a competitor's wheel hub seal. During his diagnostic review of the seal problem, the salesperson asks questions about the frequency of the current failures, the consequences and costs of a failure, and other information that helps frame the costs the customer is bearing due to the problematic seal. When the salesperson ultimately discovers the root cause of the problem and demonstrates a solution that will eliminate the problem, he is armed with the data required to dollarize his solution.

Example 2

The Heatsink Company* specializes in thermal management products for the electronics industry. Heatsink's product manager has been working with a lighting fixture company, helping it convert from a conventional ballast to a new electronic mechanism. The company has considered several options for dissipating the heat generated by the new electronic ballast and has hinted that Heatsink's design has an advantage because it weighs less than the other products being considered. The Heatsink team was initially confounded as to why weight would be a consideration. To their internal reckoning, a few ounces would not make a difference in an end user's ability to hang a light fixture from the ceiling. Heatsink's product manager persevered in his efforts to discover the dollarized value of the weight savings, probing at every opportunity. Finally, his discussion of the logistical requirements for the product bore fruit. It turned out the product will be partially assembled offshore, so the thermal management product would need to be shipped to the offshore location, and then back again after assembly. The customer has determined that the weight reduction would have significant impact on shipping costs. After

---

*The name Heatsink Company has been substituted to protect the confidentiality of the company discussed in this case study.

discovering the approximate impact on shipping savings, Heatsink was able to dollarize and justify its price premium.

Example 3

In some cases, the data development process can be an intentional collaboration between buyer and seller. Representatives from both the marketer and customer join forces to assess whether a particular project makes economic sense for both parties. This is typically accomplished only in the context of an established business relationship. Consider the experience of California Aerospace Sealants (CAS).

CAS has been a leading supplier of sealants to makers of aircraft for more than 50 years. The company has been supplying bulk sealant to a maker of regional jets for more than 10 years, and enjoys strong market share and strong satisfaction ratings with this customer. CAS has proposed switching from bulk sealant supply to a program where it would deliver ready-to-use, single-use sealant applicators for the customer's sealant operations. CAS has been successful in launching this program with other customers, delivering a solution that is truly a win-win. CAS is able to earn higher revenues and higher margins by handling tasks for which it is uniquely competent, while the customer is able to reduce internal costs and to free up resources to focus on its own core competency—building airplanes.

CAS first introduced this program just as the regional jet customer was launching its own major cost reduction initiative. The interests of the buying and selling organizations came together, with both agreeing to assemble a joint task force to assess the potential impacts of the point-of-use program. Working together, the teams identified all the potential points of impact for the project, and then proceeded to analyze the cost implications of each. The end result was a comprehensive cost reduction analysis that was jointly "owned" by both parties.

RESEARCH-DRIVEN DATA DEVELOPMENT

In situations where there is some uniformity in the way different customers use a product or service, several broad-based market research techniques can be used to develop critical dollarization data. Some of the common variations are outlined here.

Technical Data/Expert Assessment

One data development option is to look for experts who specialize in your target industry and to temporarily hire that expertise. The expert is able to act as a proxy for the target customer audience. For example, when Gladstone Pipe Coatings (see case in Chapter 6) set out to dollarize the value of its new Ultra pipe coating for petroleum pipelines, it retained a highly respected engineering firm that specializes in helping pipeline companies (Gladstone's customers) design and manage complex pipeline installation projects. This firm offered a deep technical understanding of the pipeline design and construction process, a thorough understanding of pipeline installation costs, and a broad customer perspective, as it had worked with several of Gladstone's top customers. The firm offered one other important benefit: With a respected and credible industry source writing its report, any analysis generated by the consultant would enjoy a high degree of acceptance in the marketplace.

Gladstone retained this firm to conduct a comprehensive review of the impacts of the new Ultra coating on pipeline construction. The firm studied available technical data and also created a model for comparing Ultra with other coatings on various types of pipeline projects. The work identified the key performance differences, as well as the cost implications of each of those differences. In all, more than 40 cost impacts were considered. The final report was presented in a format that could be shared with Gladstone's target customers.

Gladstone took the engineering consultant's tome and created its own pipeline economics calculator. This tool enabled Gladstone salespeople to leverage the power of the consultant's complex analysis. With a few keystrokes on a laptop, a Gladstone salesperson could generate a cost analysis for a 100-kilometer pipeline project.

Direct Customer Research

In many cases, the best place to look when seeking dollarization intelligence is the target customer base. Especially when there is sufficient homogeneity among target customers in a market (at least in terms of the usage of the subject product or service), the marketer can poll broad numbers of those customers in order to generate representative answers to the key dollarization questions.

For several years, Remsen Security Products (see detailed case in Chapter 5) struggled to develop strategies for defending its high-performing, premium-priced products against lower-priced competition. There was little doubt that the Remsen product was superior; to this most customers would readily accede. However, facing tight budgets, customers struggled to justify spending the extra money required for the apparently superior Remsen product. It was not uncommon for a hands-on locksmith who believed in the Remsen product to suggest to his purchasing colleagues that they make the extra investment in Remsen. Until recently, those pleas were futile.

After dozens of interviews with locksmiths and other industry players, Remsen ultimately designed a market research methodology that would generate the data it needed to prove its case. Remsen used a third-party research firm to poll hundreds of locksmiths, asking them to review their repair histories to gauge the relative repair frequency among Remsen and competitive brands. The results showed a demonstrable difference in Remsen's favor. The data showed, in effect, that owners of Remsen door hardware were required to repair their door hardware less frequently, and therefore spent less on maintenance (the research also collected data on typical repair costs). This data was used to develop a lifetime cost-of-ownership analysis that could be customized for any customer.

SECONDARY RESEARCH

When direct customer contact or market research does not reveal the data points required to complete a dollarization analysis, it is time to hit the books. Marketers can often find the missing pieces of their dollarization puzzles through published sources. Consider these two examples:

Example 1

Piccadilly Tools, a leading maker of pneumatic mechanics' tools, was preparing to introduce a new "smart" wrench that automatically measured and controlled the torque (or tightness) of a tire lug nut. Recognizing that tire shops with low-wage, transient workers struggled to maintain quality control, the company saw its product as a safeguard against improperly fastened automobile wheels. The "smart" wrench system required a significant investment by a tire shop, and therefore received much greater scrutiny than a normal tool purchase. Piccadilly discovered that limited data existed on the industry, so it set out to develop its own market intelligence.

Anecdotal evidence suggested that most tire shops experienced periodic wheel-off accidents, where a customer's wheel would separate from the vehicle due to improper fastening of lug nuts. Occasionally, these incidents would cause serious accidents resulting in property damage, personal injury, and even fatality (typically when the vehicle went out of control or the separated wheel struck another vehicle or pedestrian). The Piccadilly marketing team built a library of news reports, court documents, and other data to frame the costs of a single catastrophic accident. The team also conservatively estimated the frequency of such incidents by dividing the number of reported stories in a typical year by the total number of tire replacements completed each year, which were available from published industry data. This approach was considered conservative because many such wheel-off incidents were never reported.

Example 2

A computer systems consulting firm proposed a network upgrade to a regional bank. The proposal clearly outlined how the upgrade would improve transaction speed and customer service response time. The consultant struggled to find a way to connect those so-called soft benefits with real bottom-line value. Finally, the answer was found in a business journal article. The article cited a study by a major bank that concluded that every percentage point improvement in customer satisfaction resulted in an incremental $1.40 in new bank revenue per customer household.

The consultant was able to connect this financial data to the impact promised by its service offering, enabling the bank's management team to justify the six-figure investment.

INDIRECT CUSTOMER RESEARCH

As described in Chapter 2, dollarization places a monetary value on the solution to a customer problem, which can represent either the avoidance of loss, the chance for gain, or both. Most companies focus their energies on dollarizing the avoidance of loss, which is to say they focus on *cost consequences*, while paying less attention to the potential sales and marketing upside for the customer.

When a product or service offering is expected to impact the way your customer's *customers* benefit from enhancements to your customer's offering, it is useful to seek the perspective of the end market when assessing your value. Your customer's sales and marketing organizations can be a good source for intelligence here. You might ask them, for example, how a specific enhancement to their product would be received in their marketplace. You also might ask them how certain aspects of your product or service offering might help them to raise prices, attract more customers, or both.

It is important to note that marketing and sales professionals typically do not share the predatory mind-set toward vendors that is so common among purchasing professionals. The marketing team (including product managers, advertising people, salespeople, and others) will often welcome your inquiries with open arms.

But in some situations, even the customer's marketing team may not be able to provide the level of intelligence required to satisfy your data needs. In these situations, you must refocus your efforts on the end market (in effect, taking on the marketing job for the customer).

> *Note:* Your customer's channel partners, including dealers, distributors, and retailers, can also be a good source for market intelligence. They are typically more intimate with the end customer than a manufacturer is, and can shed light on the problems end customers face and on the potential impacts of improvements or changes in a product they buy.

Example

CAP Industries* is a maker of an engine component for large, over-the-road trucks. For years the company enjoyed dominant market share, price leadership, and superb brand recognition among end users (truck owners and operators).

After CAP's patent protection expired, though, competitors began to enter the market. The emerging competitors offered a me-too product and began to snipe at CAP's market share through bargain-basement pricing offers to large engine makers. With little technical differentiation to stand on, CAP turned to its traditional strength: its brand supremacy among end-use customers.

CAP's marketing challenge was figuring out how to convert that brand equity with end users into an economic argument with its direct customers, the engine makers.

CAP designed a research plan that would ask, among other questions, how much extra truck owners would be willing to pay to include CAP's device in their engines over other competitive options. The research showed that some segments of end customers would not give up CAP's product for any cost. Although

---

*The name CAP Industries has been substituted to protect the confidentiality of the company discussed in this case study.

others were indifferent—they would take whichever brand was offered by the engine maker—the overall marketplace demonstrated a strong preference for the CAP brand, with a majority of end customers willing to pay a premium of several hundred dollars over competitive brands. CAP was able to package these research findings and report to their engine-maker customers, demonstrating that the extra investment the engine maker was required to make in CAP's product (in the form of a higher price) would generate a robust return when resold to the engine maker's customers.

HYBRID APPROACHES

The examples above demonstrate how specific market research approaches can be used to identify discrete pieces of data required to complete a dollarization analysis. Of course, in many cases, multiple approaches must be used. Consider these examples:

Example 1

In the earlier smart wrench example, the marketer was able to identify the costs and relative frequencies of serious incidents caused when improperly fastened lug nuts caused the separation of a wheel from a vehicle. This data was found through a variety of published sources. A less dramatic impact of the fastening system required more traditional research, direct with the target customer audience.

Of all the occasions when a wheel is not properly fastened, only a small percentage actually result in catastrophic wheel-off accidents. When these events do occur, the costs involved are enormous, so these accidents get the lion's share of attention. A more common, though less dramatic, result of improper fastening is the increase in reworks a tire shop faces. Reworks occur when customers return to the tire shop to have past work redone, repaired, or otherwise remedied. These repairs are typically made at no cost to the customer (or said differently, without additional compensation for the tire shop).

To quantify this aspect of the new system's value, the smart wrench marketer conducted telephone and fax surveys of tire shops. The researchers asked tire shop managers to anonymously estimate the frequency of reworks, and the labor time required to make common rework repairs. They also asked for the volume of tires handled by each shop, so the data could be standardized in a per-tire format. The result was another layer of supporting data that would credibly support the economic case for an investment in the smart wrench system.

Example 2

The aircraft bearing example detailed in Chapter 7 was the result of a combination of research methods. The marketing team for the new bearing interviewed aviation industry experts *and* pored through stacks of published data to document the costs involved when flights were canceled due to an unplanned maintenance need. In making their business case, they were able to provide a comprehensive look at unplanned flight interruption costs, which created favorable credibility among their airline customers.

The marketer also faced the challenge of quantifying the *frequency* of unplanned bearing replacements. The researchers were able to develop initial estimates based on the sales volume of conventional bearings in the aftermarket, but that information contained too many variables to prove definitive. The marketing team then set out to conduct a direct research study with maintenance engineers at airlines. The study required tenacity, as airline personnel are notoriously reluctant to share data that might suggest safety risks. But ultimately, enough responses were collected to estimate a ballpark frequency rate that could then be adjusted during meetings with prospective customers.

Chapter 22

Making Dollarization Work with the Customer

Studies published in medical journals have shown that doctors with a good bedside manner face significantly fewer malpractice claims. The same is true when a sales or marketing professional introduces dollarization to a customer. Like the clinically superb physician who lacks warmth and empathy, the seller who relies only on the technical merit of dollarization analysis will face customer resistance.

Over the years, we have learned several lessons about interacting with customers when using a dollarization approach in direct face-to-face selling. The most important lesson is that the customer must be actively involved in the process. A customer who is handed a fully baked dollarization analysis *may* accept it in good faith, but more likely will see it as a ploy by the seller to justify the purchase of a product. In selling, customer participation leads to persuasion.

INVOLVING THE CUSTOMER

First it is useful to explore why customer involvement is important.

Customer Buy-in Is a Must

Dollarization without customer buy-in will not succeed. If a customer views your analysis as a self-serving tool to coax the customer into paying for your solution, that customer will likely be reticent in sharing information, will discount your claimed outcomes, and will undermine your efforts with other colleagues. An important early selling step is to help the customer understand that, as a consultative seller, you are sincerely interested in helping improve the customer's business situation. Dollarization is your tool to make sure the economic returns to the customer are acceptable.

Your Customer Can Be Your Best Salesperson

Your dollarization arithmetic and documents become a selling and closing tool. As with any closing technique, an important purpose of your dollarization work is to equip your customer contact to gain buy-in from his or her internal colleagues—the hidden decision makers. The dollarization work helps your customer contact sell in your absence.

Consequently, it is crucial that your customer understand how the total value is calculated. It is also helpful if your contact believes that the bigger the savings, the better he or she looks.

You will be making a strategic selling mistake if you try to sell the customer with your dollarized value before you have shown the customer the benefits to him or her of dollarization.

You will know you have made a mistake if your customer debates your numbers. If your customer debates the numbers downward, then you will know your customer sees your dollarization as a selling ploy, and not as a professional analysis that benefits him or her.

SELLING THE DOLLARIZATION CONCEPT

Here are the key elements to helping build credibility with the customer:

- It is generally not recommended that you try to do dollarization calculations with a customer until you have done a thorough needs analysis. In other words, do not begin assessing your potential value until you have conducted some level of diagnosis. Do not try to force-fit your solution without first finding a customer need. Gain an understanding of the problems your customers are facing, where their pain is, where their priorities are. You will not know where to focus your dollarization until you complete this step in the selling process.

- After the needs analysis, and after having determined preliminarily why you believe the customer should do business with you and your company, you are ready to sell the concept of dollarization. Some suggested steps include:

  - Let the customer know that part of your problem-solving approach will include an analysis of the financial viability of the project. This analysis is most productive when conducted jointly with your customer.

- Also let the customer know that your intention is to help him gain credit among his colleagues for any financial benefit you discover. You want your customer to be the hero. You just want the business.
- It is okay to let the customer know early on that your prices may not always be the lowest among all competitors, but that you are firmly focused on delivering the best total economic outcomes for your customers. Many customers are preprogrammed to focus first on price. You may have to educate them about the price/value relationship as outlined in this book.

When it comes time to begin working on the actual dollarization analysis with your customer, the following sequence of steps will ensure acceptance.

1. *Develop precall pro forma.* Based on your past experience and based on your needs analysis with the customer, develop a pro forma set of calculations that lead to the dollarized value of your solution, based on your current understanding.
2. *Prepare homeworked data.* Again, using your past experience, institutional knowledge, and information gained from the customer, fill in as much of your calculation data as possible before meeting with the customer (see Figure 22.1). This will give you an initial view of the robustness of the potential value of your solution, and it will help prepare you for sitting down with your customer. These numbers will be your backup in the event the customer is unable or unwilling to provide data.
3. *Ask customer for data.* Part of the ongoing buy-in process with customers is to give them every opportunity to make

Detailed Project Inputs

ENTER DETAILED PROJECT VARIABLES BELOW	Return to Major Inputs	View Detailed Calculations	Review Cost Comparisons
DEFINITIONS are provided on the HELP PAGE.	Go to HELP PAGE	Enter Other Project Costs	Print Detailed Report

	CHOOSE Baseline or Your Data	YOUR DATA	BASELINE DATA
Percentage Reduction of Mechanical Protection Allowed by Using Ultra Coating	Enter Your Own Data	15%	20%
Coating Pricing per Meter for MaxBond	Enter Your Own Data	$24.45	$25.77
Coating Pricing per Meter for Ultra	Use Baseline Data		$28.34
Number of Joints Coated per Day	Enter Your Own Data	160	140
Daily Crew Cost for MaxBond Joint Coating	Use Baseline Data		$9,000
Daily Crew Cost for Ultra Joint Coating	Use Baseline Data		$14,000
Joint Coating Materials Costs per Joint (MaxBond)	Use Baseline Data		$40.00
Joint Coating Materials Costs per Joint (Ultra)	Use Baseline Data		$52.00
Number of Small Repairs per Meter (MaxBond)	Use Baseline Data		0.2500
Number of Small Repairs per Meter (Ultra)	Use Baseline Data		0.0100
Small Repairs Completed per Hour for MaxBond	Use Baseline Data		50.00
Small Repairs Completed per Hour for Ultra	Use Baseline Data		50.00

FIGURE 22.1 This input page from a dollarization calculator illustrates the points made in steps 2 to 4. The column on the far left lists all the inputs required to complete the analysis. The column at the far right contains reference baseline data developed by the seller prior to presenting the calculator to the customer. The column titled "Your Data" allows the seller to ask for customer-specific information, which then overrides the reference data. Absent customer-supplied numbers, the calculator uses the reference data.

the dollarization analysis their own. Before meeting with a customer, prepare your calculations, but keep all the home-worked numbers to yourself (keep them handy for reference). Plan the questions you will need to ask the customer to collect the pieces of data required for your calculations, and then begin asking.

4. *Fill in with your ballparks as needed.* Always try to use a number provided by your customer. However, if the customer does not know a particular fact (or won't share it with you), you must be ready to suggest a number (based on your prior homework). You might say, "Based on our experience with similar projects, that figure is generally in the range of 50 to 75. Does that sound reasonable to you?" The customer will generally agree that your figures are close enough. Unless the customer suggests a specific number, always choose a number that will result in the most conservative result for your customer. This is not the time to over-reach. Also be sure to jointly agree to verify these estimated numbers later.

A Note on Asking Customers for Data

Salespeople frequently get nervous when we suggest that they will need to ask their customers for data that might be considered sensitive. They say, "My customer will never share that kind of information." Generally, salespeople will over-dramatize the actual customer sensitivity, but real conflicts can arise. When this issue does come up, the first thing we tell salespeople is that a customer will react in that manner only if the information is truly of a confidential nature or, more likely, if the salesperson has not yet sold the customer on the *concept* of dollarization. If the customer believes the dollarization exercise is first and foremost in the *seller's* interest, he will withhold data. If he sees that it is in *his own* best interest, he will be more forthcoming.

Further, the salesperson should consider the possible types of response he might receive if he does in fact ask.

A Note on Asking Customers for Data *(Continued)*

There are three possibilities:

1. The customer will know the answer and tell the salesperson.
2. The customer will know the answer and *not* tell the salesperson.
3. The customer will not know the answer.

If the seller gets the first response listed, he is all set. If he gets one of the other two, he must be ready with his own ballpark data to help keep the analysis moving forward. A good technique is to suggest a reasonable number and to ask the customer if he feels the number is close enough for a preliminary pass at the analysis. The customer will generally guide the seller to a fairly accurate result.

If the customer refuses to share data altogether, the seller must evaluate the root cause. If the customer does not seem to trust the seller's intentions, the seller must back off and reestablish his mission.

Of course, none of this will be known until the seller asks the first question!

5. *Always ask for agreement.* With every number that you suggest for the calculations, be sure to ask the customer for agreement. Also, make sure the customer is following your arithmetic. It is not uncommon for customers to lose track of how you are calculating specific values, and pride often prevents them from letting on that they are lost. Be sure they are with you each step of the way.

Also, when segments of your calculation are complete, review the results, and ask the customer if he feels the numbers calculated appear to be accurate. Sometimes, savings will appear so dramatic that the customer might respond, "That can't be true!" If this happens, walk through the arithmetic again, asking if there are any inputs the customer wishes to change. It may even make sense to scale back the numbers to even more conservative levels to improve the customer's comfort level.

6. *Show every calculation.* When showing your dollarization approach, be sure to make every mathematical step visible and self-evident to your customer (see Figure 22.2). It is tempting for salespeople to neatly summarize their dollarization analysis in a concise package. This is fine, as long as the detailed supporting calculations are available to the customer for reference.

   When a customer sees only the final results, two things can happen. First, because the step-by-step logic behind the results is not visible, the customer will tend to discount the validity of the final result. Second, the customer may be reluctant to share the results with colleagues because the absence of supporting detail makes it difficult for the customer to explain the methodology and answer colleague questions. The

Coating Repair Costs (During Installation)	MaxBond	Ultra		Difference
Coating Repair (Small Repairs)				
Hourly Cost of Repair Crew	$600.00	$600.00		
÷ Small Repairs Completed per Hour	50	50		
x Number of Small Repairs per Meter	0.25	0.01		
= Repair Costs per Meter (Small Repairs)	$3.00	$0.12	$	(2.88)
Coating Repair (Large Repairs)				
Hourly Cost of Repair Crew	$600.00	$600.00		
÷ Large Repairs Completed per Hour	5	3		
x Number of Large Repairs per Meter	0.01	0.0025		
= Repair Costs per Meter (Large Repairs)	$1.20	$0.50	$	(0.70)
Total Coating Repair Costs per Meter	$ 4.20	$ 0.62	$	(3.58)

FIGURE 22.2 Detailed calculations similar to these must be evident so the customer can follow the analysis and can discuss it intelligently in the absence of the seller.

customer will be unwilling to champion the results unless he is 100 percent confident he can explain how they were calculated. Step-by-step reference calculations are the "training wheels" the customer needs to create that confidence.

This issue is particularly problematic when a seller uses spreadsheet software for calculating the analysis. It is easy to embed the complicated calculations so the spreadsheet appears to magically present results upon entering inputs. It is a mistake, however, to not include the step-by-step calculations behind the results.

PRESENTING VALUE

Another consideration when working through a dollarization analysis with a customer is how to present the final results. Different selling situations call for different approaches. Following are some examples of useful formats.

Total Dollar Value

The simplest and most common approach is to simply state the gross dollar value created by the seller's solution. For example, "This program is expected to generate total savings of $240,000."

This approach is effective for headline purposes, but may not stand up to greater scrutiny. For instance, the net gain is apparent, but the investment required to achieve this investment is not. For a customer who could achieve such savings with an investment of $200, this would be truly compelling. But for a customer required to invest $20 million, the savings would be less enticing.

Effective Price

There are two variations on this approach, both of which are helpful when trying to demonstrate the total economic difference between two competing products. This approach is also particularly useful when the total value delivered is the result of purchasing multiple units of the seller's product.

This approach calls for converting the total dollarized value into "per unit" terms, and then subtracting the total per-unit value from the nominal price of the product (to yield an effective price). Conversely, the total per-unit value can be *added* to the *competitor's* unit price in order to demonstrate the true effective price for the competitor. If we have confused this simple approach, the following examples should help clarify it.

Consider a program that calls for selling 100,000 units at a price of $10 each versus a competitor whose price is $8. Assume the total dollarized value generated by the seller's solution is $500,000. (The dollarized value per unit would amount to $500,000 ÷ 100,000 units = $5.) The seller could present his value in either of the two following formats.

In Figure 22.3, the customer would compare the effective net price ($5) to the competitor's price of $8 for an apples-to-apples comparison.

APPROACH 1

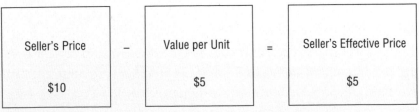

Seller's Price	−	Value per Unit	=	Seller's Effective Price
$10		$5		$5

FIGURE 22.3 Determining the Seller's Effective Price

APPROACH 2

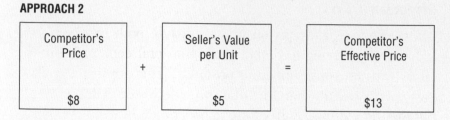

FIGURE 22.4   Determining the Competitor's Effective Price

Now consider the second variation on the same theme (see Figure 22.4).

Here, the customer would compare the competitor's effective cost per unit ($13) to the seller's price of $10. Note that either way the results are presented, the net difference in total cost per unit is the same: $3.

For planning purposes, the second method is generally safer, as it avoids one awkward result: If, for instance, the seller's total value per unit is *greater* than the seller's price per unit, the effective price for the seller becomes a *negative* number. The comparison with the competitor's nominal price still produces the correct net difference, but trying to explain a negative effective price can create unnecessary confusion.

For example, in the previous example, if the total dollarized value of the seller's solution is $1,500,000 (rather than $500,000), the dollarized value per unit would be $15. In this case, the illustrations would play out as in Figures 22.5 and 22.6.

As you can see in Figure 22.5, the seller's effective net cost per unit appears as a *negative* $5. This is still a valid analysis, but as noted previously, discussing a negative result with a customer in this scenario can complicate matters.

Meanwhile, expressing the per-unit analysis as it relates to

APPROACH 1

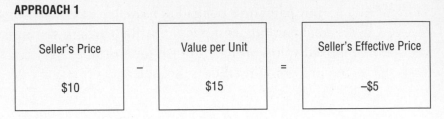

FIGURE 22.5 Determining the Seller's Effective Price (Part 2)

the competitor's cost still provides a clear and understandable result (see Figure 22.6).

As we described with Figures 22.3 and 22.4, the net difference in cost per unit is the same regardless of which approach is used. In Figure 22.5, the seller's effective price of negative $5 is compared to the competitor's nominal price of $8. The difference between the two is $13. In Figure 22.6, the competitor's effective price of $23 is compared to the seller's nominal price of $10. Again, the difference between these two values is $13.

Per Unit of the Customer's Product

In some instances, it makes sense to relate the total savings in terms of a unit of the *customer's* product. For example, an air-

APPROACH 2

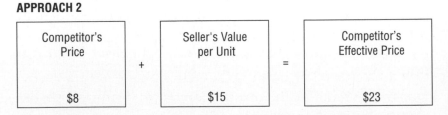

FIGURE 22.6 Determining the Competitor's Effective Price (Part 2)

craft maker may buy paint on a per gallon basis, but might be interested in the total painting cost *per plane*. Rather than stating the total dollarized value of the paint solution on a per gallon basis (as in the preceding method), the seller might report on the total value per aircraft.

Dollars per Time

As described in Chapter 7, "Shortening the Sales Cycle," it is sometimes helpful to state the total dollarized savings in a time-based format. When trying to overcome a customer's tendency to delay a decision, the seller can take the total savings and show what the customer forgoes by letting a month, week, or day pass without committing.

$50,000 per year = $12,500 per quarter
= $4,167 per month
= $1,000 per week
= $200 per day (based on 5-day workweek)
= $25 per hour (based on 8-hour workday)

Return on Investment

When a seller is competing not only with traditional competitors but also with other demands on the customer's pocketbook, it can make sense to report on the return on investment (ROI) for a program. This enables the customer to compare the rates of return for various projects under consideration. ROI is calculated by dividing the net value (net return) delivered by the seller by the investment required to purchase the seller's offering. For example, consider a project that requires an investment of $100,000. The project yields $300,000 in total dollarized benefits. The net return is the total benefit minus the investment required:

$$\$300,000 - \$100,000 = \$200,000$$

In this example, the ROI is 200 percent:

$$\$200,000 \div \$100,000 = 2.0 = 200\%$$

Return on Incremental Investment

When a seller creates incremental value when compared to a lower-priced competitor, a variation on ROI can be used. Rather than measuring net return in relation to the *total* investment in the seller's product, the seller measures the net return as compared to the *incremental* investment required over and above the investment in the competitor's product. For example, in the preceding example, the seller's solution delivers $300,000 in benefits to the customer when compared to a competitor. The seller's offering will require an investment of $100,000, but say the competitor's total price is $80,000. Here, the comparison is best calculated as in Table 22.1.

In scenario 1, the customer spends $80,000 for the competitor's offering, but gains none of the value of the solutions offered by the seller (net position = –$80,000).

> *Note:* When calculating ROI, it is important to consider not only the purchase price of the product, but also any other incremental costs that will result from choosing a particular product. For example, if special tools are required to use a product, the cost of those tools must be considered on the cost side of the ROI calculation.

TABLE 22.1 Return on Incremental Investment

	Scenario 1	Scenario 2	Difference
Incremental Value Delivered	$ 0	$300,000	$300,000
Customer Investment in Product	$80,000	$100,000	$ 20,000
Customer Position after Purchase	–$80,000	$200,000	$280,000
Return on Incremental Investment			1,400%

In scenario 2, the customer spends $100,000 for the seller's offering, but gains $300,000 in value. The customer's net position is +$200,000.

So by choosing scenario 2 over scenario 1, the customer is better off by $280,000. This gain is achieved by making an extra investment of just $20,000. The return on that incremental investment is 1,400 percent ($280,000 ÷ $20,000).

Net Present Value

When selling a product that will produce a stream of benefits over several years, some customers will be interested in the net present value (NPV) of those benefits. NPV accounts for the effect that time has on the value of money (a dollar in hand today is worth more than the same dollar promised a year or more from now) and helps customers compare different projects that each provide benefits over different spans of time. While salespeople can use financial calculators and spreadsheets to calculate NPV for projects, they should be careful not to use this type of analysis without adequate financial training.

In the following example (see Table 22.2), scenario 1 looks at a customer buying a piece of equipment that would cost $10,000

TABLE 22.2　Net Present Value

	NPV	Year 1	Year 2	Year 3	Year 4	Year 5
Scenario 1	$2,719	–$7,000	$3,000	$3,000	$3,000	$3,000
Scenario 2	$3,194	$ 800	$ 800	$ 800	$ 800	$ 800

to purchase, but would deliver $3,000 per year in savings for five years. Scenario 2 involves the company renting the same piece of equipment for $2,200 per year ($11,000 total), and still gaining $3,000 in savings (for a net annual gain of $800). At a discount rate of 8 percent, the five-year cash flows are shown in the column marked "NPV." Despite the extra $1,000 paid in rental fees, the present value of the rental approach (scenario 2) is higher than the present value of the purchase option (scenario 1).

Payback

Another time-related measure of investment strength is payback. This measures how long it will take for an investment to pay back the initial investment. A $120,000 investment that produces $10,000 in monthly savings will achieve payback after 12 months. Some customers have preset payback requirements and will not make an investment that exceeds the payback criteria. Payback is typically used in the context of assessing the return on a one-time expenditure. Table 22.3 shows a payback analysis from a value calculator used by a door hardware manufacturer.

TABLE 22.3　Payback Analysis

Incremental Investment Required to Purchase	
XYZ Corporation Hardware	$10,000
÷Total Annual Savings	$13,500
= Payback Period	0.74 Years

Chapter 23

Constructing the Customer Value File

A Customer Value File (CVF) is a detailed summary of all the benefits, services, and investments that a company provides to its customers in addition to its core product or service offering. Much of the value-added that firms provide to their customers is not apparent and goes unrecognized. The purpose of the CVF is to make customers aware of the comprehensive investment made on their behalf, and to help quantify the value of those investments. In a professional fashion the CVF presents a comprehensive economic rationale for doing business with the supplier. It endorses and supports a partnership relationship between supplier and customer, and it reinforces the customer's decision to buy from the supplier. (See Chapter 8 for more on the CVF.)

There are other important reasons to use CVFs. They educate disparate parts of the customer organization about contributions a supplier is making beyond the walls of each department. They help maintain a history with a customer. They give high-level decision makers a broad perspective on the supplier's total contribution. The CVF can overcome the loss of relationships caused by personnel turnover at the customer or supplier. Importantly, the CVF also awakens the supplier to the tremendous value customers get from the supplier company.

Whereas most of the uses of dollarization in this book are in the context of securing new business, the Customer Value File is a "keep and grow" dollarization tool. The Customer Value File keeps a deal closed, and keeps a customer a customer. It can also be used to justify a new project or help smooth the implementation of price increases. The Customer Value File is a historical snapshot and economic summary that details the true and total value the customer receives from the supplier.

Creating a Customer Value File requires a commitment of energy, time, and organizational resources. Creating the *first* CVF requires lots of patience, too.

CVF Development Guidelines

1. *Pick a single customer.* Generally, CVFs share many of the same elements from one customer to the next. Therefore, it makes sense to build a first, comprehensive document for a single customer, and then to use the lessons learned and the processes developed to guide subsequent CVF development. Invent the wheel once, then ride it again and again!

   Likewise, building the first CVF for a given customer will require a great deal of effort. Subsequent updates will benefit from the work done and lessons learned on the initial rendition.

2. *Pick a team.* Building a CVF requires insight from several different parts of your organization. Be sure to involve colleagues from all important functional areas. A broad perspective will help ensure that you capture every aspect of the relationship, and it will also help you identify sources of elusive information within your company. In some cases, com-

panies bring in retirees to provide historical perspective on the customer relationship. Other companies involve industry consultants, distributors, and other nonemployees who offer a unique expert perspective. Cast a wide net!

3. *Conduct a one-day input meeting.* Brainstorm with the team all the elements that should go into the base-case CVF document. As this list is developed, initial work should also be done to identify sources for locating all the detailed data required to document each of the elements in the report. Team members should leave this input meeting with assignments for collecting information and reporting back to a team leader.

   Table 23.1 illustrates a worksheet format that is useful in collecting and organizing the inputs during this kickoff meeting.

4. *Make it part of everyday life.* Building the first CVF can be an enormous task because much of the data required lives in disparate parts of the organization. This requires manual location and collection, which is inefficient and not much fun. If an organization is committed to maintaining and updating CVFs as an ongoing strategy for protecting business, processes should be put in place to make the commonly

TABLE 23.1 Sample Kickoff Meeting Worksheet

Data Elements	Method for Calculating or Presenting	Where to Locate Required Data	Who Is Responsible
Inventory	Average Inventory × Carrying Cost	Warehouse Database	Jim
Training Provided	Man-Days of Training × Value per Man-Day	Training Department Files	Sarah

needed information readily accessible. This may mean identifying common activities (such as technical service calls, special shipments, etc.) and automatically recording them in a dedicated customer file.

When we first developed the CVF concept, we initially named it Customer Value *File* because we asked salespeople to create a file for each key customer, and to drop a brief note into that file each time some significant event took place. That way, at the end of the year the salesperson would only need to assemble all the notes in the file and generate a report.

WHAT GOES IN A CVF?

The evidence gathered in your Customer Value File documents every single service and benefit the customer gets in return for its investment in the supplier. This type of documentation is a powerful sales tool that clearly differentiates you from the competition.

In a customer's mind, the relationship with a supplier is often reduced to a comparison of the product purchased and the price paid. Even when the actual product delivered is a small part of the total supplier offering, customers tend to limit the scope of what they think they are paying for. This is often with no malice, though in some cases it is an intentional ploy to limit the seller's bargaining power. A key function of the CVF is to document and illuminate all the benefits of the product itself, *plus* all the other elements of the relationship that benefit the customer. Importantly, it lets customers know that if they were to consider a switch to another supplier, they would be giving up much, much more than just a product in a box.

Every company will have its own unique list of items to include when compiling a CVF. The following checklist is meant to be a guide in getting started and is by no means all-inclusive.

- *Dollarized investments made on customer's behalf.* If you send a technical team to a customer plant to solve a problem and receive no direct compensation for it, your CVF should report on the cost borne by your company to provide that support. If your customer asks for samples of your product and you send them at no charge, report on the cost of the samples. Many customers (and sellers) contest that these are simply "the costs of doing business." To this we respond, "Yes, they are the costs of doing business. And they are not insignificant, so we thought you should know about them."

    Some examples:

  - Training provided to customer employees (free or discounted).
  - Technical, engineering, and other consultations.
  - Consultative work on commercial projects that are never consummated.
  - Prototype development.
  - Testing services.
  - Safety stock inventories.
  - Transaction savings.
  - Systems investments made to automate transactions, order flow, and inventory.
  - Free (or discounted) samples.
  - Capital equipment investments made on customer's behalf.

- Special services.
- Expedited deliveries.

- *Dollarized benefits deriving from investments made for customer.* Whenever possible, connect the investment made on the customer's behalf with the outcomes that result from those investments. It is important to let the customer know, for example, that your firm invested $10,000 to train 20 of the customer's employees. But *more important* is the $100,000 worth of problems solved by those employees as a direct result of the training.

- *Dollarized benefits of problems solved.* If you have solved customer problems through your core offerings and have dollarized the value of those solutions, be sure to include a summary of the savings in your CVF.

- *Special events.* In the course of nearly every buyer/seller relationship, the seller is asked to go above and beyond the call of duty to save the customer from peril. This might be a weekend call for emergency service. It might be a call to bail out a competitor who ran into production problems. Whatever events might occur, be sure to call attention to them. If you don't give yourself credit when due, who will?

- *Statistical snapshot.* An overlooked tool in key account selling is the pure power of numbers. Every CVF should include a numerical look at the business relationship. When the seller tallies various measures—the total number of shipments, on-time performance, quality performance, transactions processed, man-hours worked, and on and on—the picture that is drawn creates a powerful barrier to competition. A customer that might casually consider switching to a competitor for a lower price will often reconsider when presented with the sheer volume of activity that underpins the current relationship. In addition, when the numbers demonstrate *exceptional performance* by the seller, the customer is left to consider whether that performance could realistically be bested by a lower-priced competitor.

- *Relationship history.* Another topic to consider including in a CVF is a history of the buyer/seller relationship. In many cases, the relationship predates the current players, and the richness of the past contributions made by the seller are overlooked by the current buyer. While customers have every right to ask, "What have you done for me lately?," it does not hurt to remind them that your company has helped them make lightning strike in the past, and is prepared to make it strike again in the future.

Be Creative

The CVF is an intentionally businesslike document that supports the breadth and depth of the customer/seller relationship. However, "businesslike" does not necessarily mean it must also be dry and lifeless. In addition to the impressive factual snapshot provided by the CVF, it can also be useful to include unorthodox facts to add dimension to the story. Here are two examples:

1. *Familiar faces.* A company that provided hoses and tubing to the Coca-Cola Company developed a comprehensive CVF to detail the ongoing relationship between the two companies. Recognizing Coke's brand-worshipping culture, the tubing company included two items in the CVF that stood out. First, it announced that it had eliminated

(Continued)

Be Creative *(Continued)*

all other soft drink brands from its worldwide facilities in favor of Coke products. In addition, it had all employees of the main hose and tubing factory responsible for making product for Coke assemble outside the plant on a Saturday so a photographer could record them—with each and every employee hoisting a bottle or can of Coke. That photo graced the cover of the CVF report.

2. *Suppliers are customers, too.* It is not uncommon for a supplier to also be a customer of the company it sells to. One selling challenge that comes with the typical buyer/seller relationship is that the buyer's economic power tends to give it a controlling interest in the relationship. When compiling a CVF, a supplier that is also a customer of the target company can use that status to diminish the buyer's normal hegemony. For example, a supplier to the aerospace industry highlighted its ownership of a corporate jet (worth tens of millions of dollars) made by a major customer when building a CVF for that customer. Similarly, an engineered components maker reported in its CVF for General Motors that it had provided incentives to employees that resulted in the purchase of nearly 700 GM cars, worth millions of dollars to the customer.

Appendix

The Dollarization Doctrine: Ten Rules to Successful Dollarization

1. *Always remember "price" and "cost" are* **not the same thing.** Price is one of many costs. When convenient, buyers will discuss price as if it were the only cost. They will use the words interchangeably. Be disciplined. Don't succumb!

2. *Ask "So what?"* Don't let your sales and marketing people talk about features and benefits without answering "So what?" How do those features and benefits translate to money in your customer's pocket? What are the consequences if they do not buy from you?

3. *Let dollarization guide you.* Have you designed your product, service, and all the extras that go with them to optimize the delivery of dollarized value to your customers? A key criterion in your new product development process should be the value a product can deliver to customers. If your current offering lacks meaningful value, look for enhancements that will fill the void.

4. *Use numbers.* Resist the temptation to use words when numbers can do the job so much better. "Twenty-five percent faster" is more compelling than "much faster." "Fifty new sales" is better than "significant revenue gains."

5. *Sell the concept first.* A great dollarization story will fall on deaf ears if the customer does not first understand that the analysis is meant to help her and her organization. Worse yet, it will be viewed as a selling ploy and discounted accordingly.

6. *Show your calculations.* A unique phenomenon with dollarization selling is that a customer will follow along nodding while you explain the financial analyses that produce his savings. But after you have left, the seller will be unable to re-create the math in your absence, and this will prevent him from sharing it with his peers, which is a critical step in the commitment process. In other cases, the customer will nod politely even when lost, fearing that he will look dumb for not keeping up. Show every step in the math to make your dollarization work.

7. *Do your homework.* Before sitting down with a customer to work through your dollarization math, you will need two things: a set of the calculations that will dollarize the value points you have identified (with the numbers left blank) and a set of pro forma numbers based on homework. These numbers will be your fallback if your customer is unable to provide a piece of data.

8. *Use customer numbers.* Whenever possible, ask your customer for the pieces of information required to build your dollarization analysis. In selling, customer participation begets persuasion. Any numbers that you provide will be discounted. The customer's own numbers are indisputable.

9. *Competition will always be a downward force on your prices.* This downward force of competition will never go away, so you need opposing forces on your side. The dollarized value you create and document will counter the negative pull of competition.

10. ***Don't forget to dollarize defensively.*** If you have a customer you can't afford to lose, be sure to periodically report on the dollarized value you deliver as part of your day-to-day relationship. Don't let an information vacuum allow your customer to be tempted by the lure of a low-priced competitor.

Notes

Chapter 1 Getting Started with Dollarization

1. David Ogilvy, *Confessions of an Advertising Man* (New York: Atheneum, 1963): 99.

Chapter 2 Value Is a Number

1. Ralf Leszinski and Michael Marn, "Setting Value, Not Price," *McKinsey Quarterly* (1997, Number 1): 98–115.
2. Robert J. Dolan and Hermann Simon, *Power Pricing* (New York: Free Press, 1996): 25.

Chapter 3 Why Dollarize?

1. Robert J. Dolan and Hermann Simon, *Power Pricing* (New York: Free Press, 1996): 328.
2. Timothy Aeppel, "After Cost Cutting, Companies Turn to Price Rise," *Wall Street Journal* (September 18, 2002): A1.
3. J. Anderson and J. Narus, *Business Market Management* (Upper Saddle River, NJ: Prentice Hall, 1999): 55.

Chapter 5 Dollarization and Selling Your Price

1. J. Anderson and J. Narus, "Business Marketing: Understanding What Customers Value," *Harvard Business Review* (November–December 1998): 53.

Chapter 8 Dollarization to Protect and Keep Business

1. Harry Beckwith, *Selling the Invisible* (New York: Warner Books, 1997): 217–219.

Chapter 13   Dollarization and
Marketing Communications

1. David Ogilvy, *Confessions of an Advertising Man* (New York: Atheneum, 1963): 108.
2. Daniel Gross and the Editorial Staff of *Forbes* Magazine, *Forbes Greatest Business Stories of All Time* (New York: John Wiley & Sons, 1996): 162.
3. Ogilvy, *Confessions*, 107.

Chapter 14   Pricing New Products

1. Michael Marn, Eric Roegner, and Craig Zawada, "Pricing New Products," *McKinsey Quarterly* (2003, Number 3): 40.
2. Ibid., 40.
3. Ibid., 41.
4. Robert J. Dolan and Hermann Simon, *Power Pricing* (New York: Free Press, 1996): 80.

Chapter 15   Dollarization and
Market Segmentation

1. Vijay K. Jolly, *Commercializing New Technologies* (Boston: Harvard Business School Press, 1997): 234.
2. R. Dolan, "When Do You Know When the Price Is Right?," *Harvard Business Review* (September–October 1995).

Chapter 16   Dollarization in Consumer Marketing

1. Jane Spencer, "How Much Is Your Time Worth?," *Wall Street Journal* (February 26, 2003): D1.

Chapter 18   Dollarization and New Product Direction

1. J. Abele, B. Elliott, A. O'Hara, and E. Roegner, "Fighting for Your Price," *McKinsey Quarterly* (2002, Number 4): 116–125.

Index

Fictional company names used in the book appear in italics within this index.